Gender in the Media

Niall Richardson
and
Sadie Wearing

palgrave
macmillan

First published 2014 by PALGRAVE MACMILLAN

Palgrave Macmillan in the UK is an imprint of Macmillan Publishers Limited, registered in England, company number 785998, of Houndmills, Basingstoke, Hampshire RG21 6XS.

Palgrave Macmillan in the US is a division of St Martin's Press LLC, 175 Fifth Avenue, New York, NY 10010.

Palgrave Macmillan is the global academic imprint of the above companies and has companies and representatives throughout the world.

Palgrave® and Macmillan® are registered trademarks in the United States, the United Kingdom, Europe and other countries

ISBN 978-0-230-28473-9

This book is printed on paper suitable for recycling and made from fully managed and sustained forest sources. Logging, pulping and manufacturing processes are expected to conform to the environmental regulations of the country of origin.

A catalogue record for this book is available from the British Library.

A catalog record for this book is available from the Library of Congress.

Typeset by Cambrian Typesetters, Camberley, Surrey

Contents

Introduction: Gender and Representation

What is Sex? What is Gender?

A few years ago a rather blunt acquaintance announced that he thought gender studies was a pointless discipline and a complete waste of time. 'After all,' he said, 'we are all either male or female. What is there to discuss?' Not withstanding that there actually *is* quite a lot to discuss about whether bodies are male or female, this unenlightened acquaintance was making a commonplace error in that he was confusing gender with sex.

The foundation of gender studies is the distinction that we can draw between sex and gender. 'Sex' refers to the description of chromosomal, anatomical sex – male and female. In other words, sex is biological. Although there are cases of bodies which are intersexed, a body's sex can, for the most part, be (relatively) easily determined as it is decided by chromosomal, anatomical detail.

Gender, unlike sex, is not biological but cultural. 'Gender' refers to masculinity and femininity and describes learned patterns of behaviour or performance. Therefore, what makes a person male or female is grounded in biology and, in that respect, is universal. How a person performs or does masculinity and femininity is cultural and as such may vary according to culture or context. What is deemed appropriate femininity or masculinity in one age or culture may be entirely different from the performance expected of women or men in contemporary, Western culture. To use some obvious examples, in 18th-century Western culture it was deemed appropriate for both sexes, male and female, especially people of the higher social echelons, to wear heavy, lead-based make-up and voluminous powdered wigs. In other words, for a man to wear obvious make-up was considered an appropriate perform-ance of masculinity within that specific cultural context. Similarly, men would wear extremely ornate clothes, often exposing their legs, wear high heels and move in a theatrical, flamboyant fashion. This was considered appropriate masculinity. In contemporary culture, such a performance would usually be considered feminine and inappropriate for a male body.

The point is that these ideas of what makes appropriate masculinity and appropriate femininity do not simply happen. We don't automatically know how to behave and represent ourselves simply because of our biological sex. Instead, we learn acceptable patterns of behaviour from our culture. This is why, when people ask about the gender of a new born baby, they are asking an inappropriate question. Babies are not gendered. They are certainly sexed (male or female), but because they have had no interaction with culture they are not yet performing gender. In a similar fashion, it would be ridiculous to ask about a baby's social class identification as, once again, social class is a cultural construct which comes from integration within a cultural regime.

However, as we all know, many parents evidence a desire to make the baby's gender visible to everyone – not least in the colour coding of the baby's clothes. A boy *should* be dressed in blue and a girl in pink – or so culture tells us. This almost paranoid obsession with gendering the baby, making the baby's gender evident for everyone to see, is the first step in a lifelong commitment to maintaining gender propriety. Without necessarily being fully conscious of it, parents police their children's gender, teaching them from an early age what is deemed appropriate femininity and masculinity. For example, while both boys and girls may be given toy dolls to play with the girl's dolls will either be babies, thus teaching her the role of maternal nurturing, or fashion dolls (the most famous is 'Barbie') with which the girl child will learn the importance of grooming and making-up the body. The boy child will also be given dolls to play with but his will be action dolls – soldiers or super-heroes – with which he will be encouraged to dramatise fights and battles. Commonplace occurrences in public playgrounds (the one described here was witnessed by one of the authors of this book) exemplify this kind of gender socialisation. Two children – a boy and a girl – have dolls to play with. The boy is playing with his action figures and dramatising a veritable blood-bath in which one action figure pulverises the other, to the point where the victorious doll is jumping on the loser doll – the boy smashing the doll up and down to crush the losing doll to a pulp. The mother is witnessed applauding this and telling her son how wonderful he is. The female child had been playing happily with her baby doll (it was one of those dolls that can suck, with loud squelches, on a dummy) but, when the girl saw the 'fun' of her brother's game, she wanted to join in with the fighting and clobbering of his dolls. The mother, however, intervened to stop this and the girl child was reminded that she should play with her suckling baby doll instead.

This policing of strict gender roles continues into educational establishments where school playgrounds become veritable courtrooms, where appropriate gender roles are judged. This is particularly the case in relation to masculinity in which schoolboys will viciously (often brutally) police performances of masculinity in their peers. Any schoolboy who dares to perform something which is identified as feminine risks suffering the most intense bullying as his colleagues attempt to redirect him to the 'appropriate' gender role (see Chapter 2).

The key point here is that we all *learn* from various cultural institutions – family, friends, school – how to perform masculinity (if we are sexed as male) and how to perform femininity (if we are sexed as female). Ideas of masculinity and femininity do not just happen – they do not just automatically come from inside us – rather, we learn these from culture.

However, a great many people (and we would argue that this is the majority of the population who have not taken a gender studies course) believe that gender is simply inherent or innate. A stock phrase in Western culture is 'boys will be boys' or 'girls will be girls'. It is believed that feminine acts simply happen because a body is female while male bodies will automatically perform masculinity. Culture consistently reduces culturally acquired gender performances to simple biology.

Let's take an interesting example here. For many years, women were described as the 'gentle sex' who were delicate and more fragile than men. This was most obvious when we considered the act of swooning or passing out at times of anxiety or crisis. This was particularly popular in the Victorian era when women were, apparently, *always* swooning and fainting. This was explained by a medical discourse which diagnosed these feminine acts as something inherent in the female body. These were known as acts of hysteria and were deemed to be the direct result of having a female body. The Greek word for 'womb' is *hysteron* and 'hyster-ia' means a wandering or loose movement of the womb. The theory was that when a woman became hysterical, her womb had started to move about the body and required the intervention of the (somewhat vile) 'smelling salts' to drive the ill- disciplined womb back down into the right place. Hence we have endless representations in art and period costume dramas of swooning women crying out for their smelling salts. The key point here is that this feminine act of hysteria/swooning was deemed an essential aspect of femininity – it happened because a woman was sexed as female and had a womb.

However, the real reason why women were swooning and fainting had absolutely nothing to do with their sex – the anatomical details of their bodies – but instead was purely cultural. The culprit for many of the cases of Victorian swooning was, as is now widely known, the corset. This unpleasant device was used to enhance the woman's waist by lacing her up tightly, in what was basically a very broad whalebone belt, so that her waist size was greatly diminished. This created the highly fashionable hourglass figure. The problem, however, was that her diaphragm was greatly constricted and she could barely draw a breath, let alone a full lung of air, resulting in swooning and fainting. They were 'delicate' or the 'gentle sex' because they could barely breathe let alone engage in strenuous activity. The key point about the fashion of Victorian corsetry is that it demonstrates how something which society deemed to be essentially feminine – women were thought to be naturally delicate and given to swooning – was, in fact, a cultural construct created by the practice/regime of wearing tight corsets. The swooning Victorian woman is a prime example of how society attempts to reduce a cultural practice to a sexed, biological trait.

Although we no longer have such extreme acts as corseting bodies (apparently the corset could cause all sorts of damage to the constricted internal organs – often squashing them or causing them to dislodge from their correct place) we do still continue to 'excuse' cultural practices by deeming them to be biological traits. For example, the phrase 'boys will be boys' is generally used to excuse male violence and acts of physical aggression, such as when two teenage schoolboys leave each other with black eyes and bloody noses. One common 'biological' account for this stems from the fact that boys have more testosterone than girls and that testosterone is thought to inspire aggression. However, although it is correct that hormonal changes in the body can have a direct effect upon a person's mood, *aggressive* acts are something which a young male learns. It is true that the pubescent boy's burgeoning levels of testosterone do, indeed, affect his mood and sense of temperament, but the point is that he is more likely to manifest these emotional changes through acts of violence because he has *learned* to express himself in this way from cultural activities that are deemed appropriate for a man (as in the case of the action dolls usually given to a little boy). If a woman is distraught or anxious, her hormones in a state of flux, she is more likely to demonstrate this anxiety through crying or weeping because she has learned from culture that crying is the appropriate way for a woman to demonstrate distress or anxiety. However, a boy is taught from an early age that men are not supposed to cry so the only outlet which is available for his surge of hormonal emotion is the typical act of violence which will, of course, be explained by recourse to biological make-up: 'boys will be boys'.

To summarise the main points: 'sex' refers to male/female and is grounded in biological, anatomical details. 'Gender' refers to masculinity/femininity and describes how a person acts out specific performances or roles which are deemed, by contemporary culture, to be appropriate for male or female bodies. Of course, it is the very fact that gender *is* cultural, rather than fixed by biology, which makes it such a precarious identification and why we learn that we must constantly worry about our gender performances in everything we do. Adult life is a constant stream of anxiety related to our gender performance: am I dressed appropriately? Am I too feminine or too masculine? How do I sit in a public place such as a bus or a train? If I'm a man should I dominate the space and sit with my legs apart? If I'm a woman should I keep my legs together and contract into the space made available? Underpinning all of this for many of us are the dark memories of schoolyards in which young girls are ostracised from their peers for liking 'masculine' sports and boys are bullied and even beaten up because they like singing or the performing arts.

Arguably, this demonstrates that gender studies, far from being a 'waste of time', should actually be mandatory on the National Curriculum and perhaps we would then have much less schoolyard bullying. But we may have a few years to wait for that.

Gender and Representation

In the previous section we have argued that our ideas of what it means to be masculine or feminine do not simply happen because of our biological sex but are formed through cultural activities/practices. We learn what is deemed appropriate femininity or masculinity from parents, friends, social engagements and school. However, there is another highly influential cultural practice within Western culture: the media. Indeed, if there is one source where we really learn what is 'appropriate' masculinity or femininity it is through media representations.

We live in a world where we are assailed by media representations. Television, advertising, film, the press, the internet and new technologies which allow us to view images everywhere, such as the iPhone, all ensure that we are enthralled by media images. For many of us, our understanding and learning of what is deemed appropriate femininity or masculinity is enhanced and ensured through media representations. When thinking critically about media representations we have two key areas which we need to bear in mind. Firstly, representation is always re-presentation. In other words, the images that we see are not simply a reflection or a mirror of the world but are constructs – images which have been built or produced. As such, representations are never 'innocent', they never simply happen, but are always constructed in accordance with specific politics or ideologies. The producer of the image has coded the imagery within the text in order to produce specific meanings and often these meanings are not simply the vision of the producer but are in accordance with dominant ideologies of the period. For example, let's take a very commonplace representation, an image which most people will be familiar with: the wedding photograph.

Firstly, we should stress that this is a re-presentation of a happy, newly formed alliance between two families. Marriage is not only a bonding of two people but the union of two different family groups. Both sides of the family are re-presented as joyous on this wedding day. In reality there may be some family members who were feeling distinctly unwell or perhaps despised the person they are standing beside. The key point, though, is that they are re-presented as happy on this joyous occasion. Another issue to remember in representation studies is that a particular type (or genre) of image will always adhere to specific conventions which allow the viewer to make sense of that image. For example, the bride and groom are positioned at the centre of the image: this is a generic expectation which allows the spectator to identify the people represented. Even though the bridesmaid's dress looks similar to the bride's dress, we are able to identify the bride because she is centre stage.

However, even though this is a simple, everyday image there is a specific set of politics being expressed in the coding of the image. Marriage is about the bonding of a heterosexual couple and it is anticipated that this couple will produce a family of their own and that their children will, in turn, go on to marry and produce a family. If we look closely at the coding of the image, we can see that this specific politics of heterosexuality is expressed in the iconography. The little flower girl and page boy stand directly in front of the wedding party and look like mini-versions of the bride and groom. This mini-version of the happy couple is not only suggesting the importance that culture places upon producing children within a marriage but also indicates that it is expected that these children will then progress to marry as well and produce children of their own. Even though this is a simple, everyday image, it emphasises and affirms the politics of heterosexuality, marriage and reproduction.

This little example is helpful for simply stressing the political importance of representation in contemporary culture. For us, the authors, and for those who work in the critical study of media and culture, one of the least helpful remarks that someone can say is the dismissive phrase 'it's *only* a representation' or 'it's *only* a film/TV programme'. Media images not only represent specific ideologies but help to support these ideologies in contemporary culture. This is most important when we consider the representation of gender in the media. The media gives us a sense of what it means to be masculine or feminine and how we should enact these performances. Although there are more representations now in contemporary media of people who challenge or 'queer' traditional gender performances (see Chapter 3), the media is still emphatic in adhering to a strict regime of traditional gender in the majority of its representations.

This brings us to the second key aspect which must be remembered when we consider media representations: the sense of representation *as* representative of a specific group; an image which is 'standing in for' a specific group of people. To use another commonplace example: on every university degree course there will be a student who is entitled 'the student rep'. This student represents or stands in for the entire student body. He or she is the representation of the students' views/opinions at faculty meetings. Obviously, this is a very important job as the student rep can distinctly colour and influence the perception that the faculty has of the entire student community. For example, if the student rep is combative and rude, then this will influence the perception that the faculty have of the whole student body. In other words, this one student has to bear the burden of representation in that he or she is standing in for the entire student community.

This is particularly important when we consider representations in the media, especially when we consider that a number of representations may be of small, minority groups which are not widely known. The representation of disability is a key example in that many of the spectators may never have met anyone with the specific disability that is represented on the screen. Therefore, the only source of information which that spectator has to go on – his or her whole perception of what it means to identify with that specific disability – is shaped by the media representation. Another important example is the representation of gays and lesbians in the media given that there may well be spectators who have absolutely no knowledge of gay culture and so simply believe that the representations they see are reality.

Obviously, these are two quite specific examples and the representation of gender is not entirely comparable given that, unless the spectator is living on a desert island, he or she will encounter men and women on a daily basis. If the spectator watches an image of a hysterical, screeching woman, he or she will negotiate that image in relation to the actual women that he or she is meeting on a daily basis. Unlike, say, the representation of a person with cerebral palsy, the spectator will have met actual women and may have more appreciation of the ways that the representation is working in relation to some specific set of narrative conventions or genre expectations. In this way gender representations do not bear quite the same 'burden' of representation as those of other marginalised groups.

Nevertheless, this is not to say that media representations are not highly influential. For instance they convey an idea of what is deemed to be 'desirable' gender to the spectator. The male hero of the Hollywood film will always conform to a specific type of masculinity. It is very rare, for example, to find an effeminate man in the role of the Hollywood hero. However, it is not at all rare to find the evil villain of the film represented as effeminate and so imparting a specific gender politics: male effeminacy is evil, undesirable and, like the villain of the film, should be destroyed. In other words, the media gives us a sense of what gender performances are deemed acceptable and, more importantly, desirable, and which should be avoided.

A key strategy within media representation is the technique known as 'stereotyping'. Stereotyping works by taking a trait which *may* apply to a small minority of a group and representing it as indicative of the whole group. For example, a common media stereotype is the dumb blonde. The point to remember is that this stereotype is not necessarily inaccurate. There are a great many people in the world who are blonde and there are a great many people in the world who are as Marilyn Monroe puts it in *Some Like It Hot* 'not very bright'. Therefore, the simple law of averages dictates that there will indeed be a great many blonde people in the world who are rather 'dumb'. However, how media stereotyping works is that it suggests that *all* blonde women are dumb and hence provides the spectator with an easily recognisable, stock character that can be employed within the media text.

Stereotypes are not necessarily negative (that the French are good cooks is a stereotype and certainly not a negative one), but stereotypes are concerned with a power dynamic in that they 'pigeonhole' certain people – usually minorities – into specific categories. This is particularly important in relation to gender when we consider that many stereotypes are extremely sexist and promote gender prejudice. The stereotype of the 'dumb blonde', for example, reinforces the perceived notion of blonde women as silly, childlike and sex objects. Usually gender stereotypes work by suggesting that a physical characteristic, an aspect of gender performance, is suggestive of a much more political trait. The effeminate man is a good example here as effeminacy has, in the history of media representation, often been conflated with other less desirable qualities such as evilness or other socially unacceptable characteristics. Even a contemporary, gay-affirmative sitcom such as *Will & Grace* furthers the stereotype of effeminacy as 'bad' through its representation of the effeminate Jack. Not only is Jack's effeminacy a source of entertainment in itself (he is doing 'unacceptable' masculinity), but he is also unemployed, utterly useless and sponges off friends and family for any money he can get. In this respect, Jack's gender performance (his effeminacy) is conflated with work-shy laziness and lack of talent. The key point, therefore, to remember about stereotypes is that they not only provide a shorthand, an easy way of recognising a specific type in the text, but they can promote sexism or gender prejudice by conflating specific politics with a specific physical trait. In the case of *Will & Grace's* Jack, effeminacy stands in for his work-shyness and lack of talent. In this respect, we would argue that the study of gender in the media is a fascinating topic and one which we hope all students will enjoy.

Contents of the Book

The book is divided into two parts. The first part, 'Questions of Theory', will outline the main critical and cultural theories in the study of gender. The second part, 'Media Case Studies', will show how these critical/cultural paradigms can be applied to contemporary media, including television drama, magazines, celebrity culture, make-over shows and online/web media.

Chapter 1 introduces students to feminist cultural theory and its critical application to the study of media images. The earliest form of feminist criticism challenged the (stereo) types of women deployed by the media, arguing that women were trivialised, erased and objectified by media representations. Psychoanalytically informed work from the same period looked at the ways that sexual difference was implicated in structures of viewing, whilst work from a cultural studies perspective sought to engage with some of the pleasures offered by engaging in feminine identifications and female genres. We will also consider the recent discussions of media as embedded in a post-feminist climate, with its emphasis of playfulness and irony. We will assess how these insights can be applied in the critical study of contemporary media representations.

Chapter 2 introduces students to the other side of the gender binary: masculinities. Here we will stress the political difference in studying masculinity from femininity as, unlike femininity, masculinity has not required a political formation in order to advance its rights. Indeed, until recently men have had the luxury of not even having to consider themselves as gendered in a similar fashion to how Caucasians have not had to consider themselves raced. We consider the key strategies in the representation of masculinity and how the masculine body can bear the burden of objectification in still and moving images. We will consider recent trends in masculinity which have been represented in media texts such as 'New Laddism'. In doing so, we consider masculinity's anxiety about femininity and, more importantly, effeminacy – often termed 'effeminophobia'. Finally, we explore the speculative claims for 'metrosexuality' and ask if recent media images, especially advertising, are addressing this cultural trend.

These two chapters concern masculinity and femininity as a fixed binary system. In Chapter 3 we introduce students to the key debates within contemporary queer theory, outlining the work of Judith Butler and Eve Kosofsky Sedgwick, and how they challenge the idea of a simplistic two gender system. In her famous book, *Gender Trouble*, Butler argued that gender is a performative effect, a collection of acts or 'doings' which, within a recognised social system, creates the illusion of a fixed gender identity. Many 'queer' images – including many contemporary media images – denaturalise this seemingly fixed gender identity and demonstrate that gender is a 'doing'. There is nothing behind the actions or doings themselves; it is these actions or doings which create the impression of a gender identity. If gender is performative then it is a flexible construct and limiting gender into the binary system of masculinity and femininity seems reductionist.

However, queer theory moves a stage beyond feminist criticism by considering that if gender is regarded as the scaffold for sexual attraction (heterosexuality is the sexualisation of the masculine/feminine binary) then exposing its performative nature challenges heterosexuality's assumed naturalness. Sedgwick develops Butler's thesis further by asking whether gender is necessarily the defining attribute in eroticism. Perhaps some people eroticise a specific sensation or activity rather than the gender of the sexual partner. These debates, and the issues raised in the previous two chapters, will be further elaborated in the analyses of various case studies in contemporary media texts.

Part II develops these cultural debates further by applying these paradigms in the critical study of contemporary media. In Chapter 4 we explore how television has seen the rise of 'quality' dramas which, due to their high production values, have been described by various critics as 'cinematic television'. Many of these shows have already been the source of much critical writing in various edited collections and journal articles. However, while the aesthetics of these shows may have captivated many film critics, the interesting gender politics raised by many of the representations also deserves attention. In this chapter we consider the award winning drama *Sex and the City* and apply the cultural debates raised in Chapter 1 to a critical analysis of the show.

Ten years on from its final broadcast *Sex and the City* demands attention as one of the first of a collection of television dramas to articulate a complex image of post-feminism. *Sex and the City* has been embraced by some critics as potentially uniting feminism's goals with the playfulness, irony, embrace of glamour and critical self-reflexivity of post-feminism. Although criticised for its exclusive focus on white, middle-class identity, *Sex and the City* captured a particular post-feminist dynamic of aligning femininity with feminism (suggesting that a feminist identification need not signal a rejection of feminine iconography) . The show is also interesting for its adoption of some elements of 'queer' (as explored in Chapter 3) into its narrative. Not only did the show celebrate an adoption of elements of a queer lifestyle, in that the four women had innumerable sexual partners yet maintained a sense of support from their colleagues and community, but it was one of the first to explore the dynamics of heterosexuality. Nearly every episode featured some 'perversity' which asked the spectator to reconsider the idea of 'normative' heterosexuality. We go on to consider recent directions in 'quality drama', with particular reference to *Desperate Housewives* and the highly acclaimed series *Mad Men*, a show which arguably has a more complex 'gendered address' than *Sex and the City* and which swaps playful irony with a darker and more ambivalent current of gender politics.

In Chapter 5 we consider the make-over show – once a 'section' tagged on to morning television but which has now attained prime-time viewing. In this chapter we consider two different shows which have achieved considerable popularity: *Ten Years Younger* and *How to Look Good Naked*. *Ten Years Younger* has attained much interest for its particularly invasive and often punitive approach to its models. Unlike other make-over shows which simply revise hair, clothes and make-up, *Ten Years Younger* subjects its participants to often extensive cosmetic surgery in the attempt to make these disobedient women conform to acceptable ideas of feminine iconography. Drawing upon a Foucauldian perspective, we will consider how the show reinforces the metaphor of the panopticon prison system in which the inmate learns that she is always under surveillance and is bullied into adhering to conventional gender propriety. We speculate on how the pursuit of youth and beauty can be read as a form of 'religion' and we finish with some speculations on the more recent make-over show *How to Look Good Naked*. This show may be a less invasive, aggressive format but we will consider whether it is simply cloaking the finely tuned misogyny apparent in other make-over programmes.

One key development in gender studies has been the recent interest in body image. While the body was once theorised as a 'given' – something fixed and essential – we now view the body as something which is constructed and regimented by culture. As we've seen already in the case of make-over shows, contemporary culture evidences an obsession with a regimentation of body image, policing subjects into appropriate iconography. In short, there cannot be an interpretable body without the culture which both inscribes and also reifies it.

In Chapter 6, 'Celebrity Bodies and Lifestyle Magazines', we will be examining the ways in which the discourses of celebrity culture offer insights into questions surrounding the body. Drawing on work which has argued that celebrity offers a way of understanding 'how we are human now'(Dyer 2004: 15), we examine what this means for the forms of gendered embodiment on offer in 'celebrity culture'. What do stories about celebrities tell us about the values, affects and meanings attached to particular bodies? What sorts of pleasures are on offer in the rituals of scanning the body of a celebrity for minute changes in gendered bodily presentation? Celebrity coverage in magazines in particular offers a rich terrain for exploring the values and meanings attached to particular embodiments, ranging from questions of sexuality to the ubiquitous and contradictory discourses on slenderness.

The previous chapters consider media texts which have reinforced traditional gender roles and also some which have challenged or queered these same roles. Drawing upon feminism, masculinity studies and queer theory, Chapter 7 looks at interactive media in the shape of one of the most popular of contemporary pursuits: online dating. The rise in online dating galleries – both gay and straight – have increased in the past few years, with more and more people arranging dates in this way. However, creating a profile on these galleries is quite a constrictive activity, given that there are usually limited options with which to identify. Body types are carefully policed through a range of limited options in which the most 'desirable' conform to very conservative prescriptions of masculinity and femininity. In this chapter we will consider the politics of contemporary dating galleries and analyse how the participants 're-present' themselves – with a particular focus on how they 'perform' their gender. Indeed, the number of participants who actively attempt to challenge normative ideologies of masculinity and femininity in their own profiles seem to be very few. Even more remarkable is the horror expressed in the profiles about meeting someone who violates traditional gender roles.

Whether we are appalled, horrified or simply downright enraged by the representation of gender in contemporary media we cannot help but continue to be intrigued by it and we hope this short book will convey to students a sense of how fascinating we have found these debates to be.

Questions of Theory

1 Feminisms

Introduction: Feminist Media Studies – 'Making the invisible Visible'

It is always important to start any discussion of feminism with a reminder that it is not a single entity agreed on in advance by those who identify as feminists, be they activists or academics (a far from simple distinction). Rather, feminism should be understood as an area of contestation and debate. It is an arena of fraught arguments over the social and symbolic meanings attached to gender and sexuality as well as to race, class, age, ability and so on. What unites feminist perspectives on a very wide range of issues – from the ratio of women in governments, to questions of employment rights and rewards, to reproductive health, to debates over sex work or gender violence – is a concern to interrogate existing gender relations, identities or norms with a view to the potential for these to change and transform. 'Second-wave feminism' is the term frequently used to mark a period of activist, transformative, feminist engagement, occurring in distinct ways in the USA, the UK and Europe, which has reshaped the cultural and political status of women in these geographical areas. Feminist theory is also very clear that distinctions need to be made *between* women, such that one of the first questions a contemporary student needs to ask is 'which women' and 'where' rather than assuming that the category is self-evident. Feminists are interested in questions of justice and inequalities but also in the question of difference. As Liesbet Van Zoonen puts it, despite the differences amongst feminist approaches in different contexts:

> Some common concepts … distinguish feminism from other perspectives in the social sciences and the humanities. Its unconditional focus [is] on analysing *gender* as a mechanism that structures material and symbolic worlds and our experiences of them … This is not to say that such a focus will always result in the conclusion that gender is the defining factor … Ethnicity, sexuality, class and a range of

> other discourses intersect with gender in various and sometimes contradictory ways.
>
> (Van Zoonen 1994: 3)

For feminist *media* scholars too, the area is marked less by a single line of interest and more by a consensus that media is gendered. In other words gender is significant in production, reception and institutional contexts, as well as in relation to representational and symbolic practice. Feminist scholars of media come from a variety of disciplines. In addition to media and communications, the field has been marked by the input of sociologists and literary, film, television and cultural studies scholars. Moreover, it is also an area of significance to those working within the media industries. Importantly too, as Hollows and Moseley (2006) suggest, feminism is also experienced and encountered by audiences *through* popular culture. All of these perspectives share the understanding that gender matters in relation to media.

An introduction of this type cannot hope to offer a comprehensive analysis of all the work which takes a feminist approach to media, but the sketch that follows is designed to introduce some of the key debates which have structured the field, including key areas of representation, symbolic function and reception.

Annette Kuhn suggests that it is helpful to regard feminism as a 'frame of reference or a standpoint' or 'as a set of conceptual tools and a method or series of methods' (Kuhn 1994: 68). Whilst these are conceptually distinct, they need to be thought of together. One distinction is whether scholarship employs a sociological or a humanities influenced approach. A sociological analysis can be identified as the 'images of women' approach in that it considers the political importance of representations of women, especially in relation to how these images can be seen to 'reflect' the position of women in the real world. By contrast, the approaches derived from literary criticism and film theory are more likely to consider the ways that mediation works in relation to representation and to attend to questions of ideology and social construction using methods and theories from semiotics, structuralism and psychoanalysis. These debates could be labelled the 'women *as* image' approach.

These distinctions and differences between feminist methods and theories are linked through a feminist perspective. Different groups have different investments in the analysis of gender and media. Those working within the industry have a very different relationship to it than those immersed in theoretical debate. However, what these different perspectives do share is a concern with the politics of gender and sexual relations (including exclusions and injustices) in relation to the media industries and its products. They contest and critique, in different ways, the existing structures and regimes of media. What unites feminist analysis is the desire to 'make visible the invisible' (ibid.: 71) at the levels of text, production and context.

Questions surrounding the relationship between representation and the social world have been key issues for feminists whose interest is predicated on the assumption that the media are powerful and influence the ways in which we all experience gender. This, in part, relates to the key insight, outlined in the Introduction, that biological sex and cultural gender can be understood as distinct, and that the media is part of the process through which gender accrues meaning. French feminist philosopher Simone de Beauvoir argues in *The Second Sex* that one is not 'born woman' rather one is 'made'. This idea, that biological sex (how one is born female) should be understood as distinct from what one becomes – gender (woman) – means that the distinction between female and feminine is a crucial insight for feminism. (More recently this sex/gender distinction has been subject to criticism as various philosophers have argued that sex itself is also constructed and produced via culture and within matrices of power (Butler 1990).) Nonetheless, despite these qualifications it is hard to over estimate the importance of the idea that femininity and masculinity are historically and culturally variable, and also that they are raced (Truth 1995; hooks 1996) and classed (Skeggs 2004). As stressed in the Introduction, the media are implicated in the ways that masculinity and femininity are constructed, maintained and transformed and analysis of this process is a key aspect of feminist media debate.

Representations: Images of Women

Media and cultural imagery of women came to be seen as one of the key sites for feminist engagement in the 1970s. During this period activists, as well as academics, raised questions about representation which are still pertinent and the subject of much popular gender debate today. Why are women's bodies used so extensively to sell things? What are the dominant and dominating images associated with femininity? What role do the media play in ascribing and regulating prescriptive gender roles? Traditional versions of masculine and feminine roles and identities can easily be identified in contemporary media culture – scatterbrained women still angst about their appearance and vie for 'Mr Right' (e.g. the *Bridget Jones* franchise and many other 'chick flicks'), while (super) heroes are still overwhelmingly male. Of course some imagery is changing but, for the most part, gender in the mainstream media is still largely understood as dichotomous and, as we saw in the Introduction, is part of the socialization of both men and women.

In 1978 Gaye Tuchman famously described the representation of women in the mass media as 'symbolic annihilation' (Tuchman et al. 1978: 8), noting that 'relatively few' women were portrayed at all and when they were they were generally confined to being either a 'child like adornment' or a dutiful housewife. Where they did appear as 'working women' they were 'condemned' or 'trivialised'. The sex role stereotyping that was uncovered through this kind of research found plenty of evidence to support the view that the media was complicit in upholding unequal relations between men and women through the stress placed on keeping women in the private sphere of home and the domestic, whilst men performed the public roles. For feminists this public/private distinction is understood as a key problem to be analysed and broken down, rather than something inevitable or natural, hence the slogan 'the personal is political'. Feminist engagement in debates over popular culture in this early period were particularly interested in contesting the dominance of particular versions of femininity and a key and much cited text here is Betty Friedan's *The Feminine Mystique*. She argued that the idealisation and manufacture (in large part through the media) of the feminine suburban middle-class white norm fostered deep unhappiness in women whose lives were constrained by such limited ambition (2001). Of course, Friedan's critique comes from a quite privileged and limited perspective. Nonetheless, it is an important and very influential text and the primacy it accords to the white, middle-class norm is close to the perspective of many of the commentators on gender in the press, even today, as we will see in the discussion of *Mad Men* in Chapter 4 (see pp. 78–80). The predominance of this image of femininity then, as passive, pretty and dependent, still has relevance.

Tuchman uncovered the relative invisibility of women in media representation. Her analysis showed a numerical bias in favour of the representation of men. We might fondly imagine that things have changed a great deal since the 1970s. Unfortunately, however, the reality is depressingly consistent. The Centre for the Study of Women in Television and Film publishes detailed statistics and reports on the roles of women within the film and television industry, both behind and in front of the camera. Their findings show that women are still under-represented in all aspects. Films which do feature women have routinely lower budgets, open in fewer cinemas and are screened for less time (Lauzen 2008). In 2011 only 33 per cent of characters in the 100 highest grossing US films were female and only 11 per cent were lead protagonists, a decline from 16 per cent in 2002, demonstrating that progress in this area is far from a given (Lauzen 2012). Furthermore, the kind of representation is also far from gender neutral, with men more likely to be offered 'leadership' roles than women, which the author of the report accounts for in part because she also notes that female characters tend to be younger than male characters, with 50 per cent of male characters being over 40 as opposed to 25 per cent of female. These statistics are also mirrored in the way that films are made, with only 18 per cent of the production workforce (directors, executive producers, writers, cinematographers and editors) of the 250 highest grossing US films of 2012 being female (Lauzen 2013), while women made up a miserable 9 per cent of the most revered role in cinema – the director. While the question of the gender of the cinematic gaze has preoccupied critics and theorists for a long time (see the discussion of Mulvey below) these statistics are a stark reminder that the questions which preoccupied the feminist commentators of the 1970s – who is responsible for the representations that surround us, and how are they gendered? – are questions that still need to be asked despite the success of films like *Bridesmaids* or *The Heat* which might suggest that women have equal access to the screen.

The problem identified with the kind of research that looks at images of women is that it can tend to rather oversimplify the question of the image itself. It also positions feminist critics as 'outsiders' looking on and judging popular culture, and it has consistently been called to task for its dependence on a 'hypodermic' model of communication which not only sees women as passive dupes of ideology, who lack the critic's superior ability to see through stereotypical imagery, but which has also failed to take women's enjoyment of popular culture seriously (Hollows and Moseley 2006: 4). Calls for 'realistic images' in place of idealised or demeaning ones won't solve the problem because reality is more complex and women more heterogeneous than any 'corrective' image can hope to account for. Critics argue that it may well be useful to think about the way that particular groups are represented through stereotypes because of what this reveals about the systematic nature of oppression and because it stresses the potentially profound psychic and social consequences for individuals. However, they also suggest that analysis based on stereotype runs very serious risks of reproducing rather than contesting these constructs (Shohat and Stam 1994). Van Zoonen reminds us that engagements with media which critique images for being stereotypical or unrealistic are based on a premise that gender itself is simple and the result of a straightforward distinction, whereas the reality is more complex (see Carter and Steiner 2004: 14).

As will be discussed later in this chapter, media scholarship on gender has, over the past two decades, taken seriously some of the genres explicitly aimed at women. This has been considered important, not least because those genres associated with the 'feminine' were often dismissed as trivial and unworthy of scholarly attention. Women's magazines are one such area, and we will take this up in Chapter 6 through a discussion of celebrity; but it is worth noting here that women's magazines stage an important aspect of the reproduction of femininity within capitalist society (a link also returned to in Chapter 4 in relation to television drama and in Chapter 5 in relation to the make-over show). Femininity in women's magazines is often figured as something which basically needs 'work', constant maintenance and the injection of lots of money. Also of note is the fact that magazines rely on advertising to sustain production which makes them vulnerable to editorial pressures (ibid.: 180). Prescriptive ideas about the ideal feminine body (as well as about job, house and other lifestyle elements that magazines routinely pronounce on) have been criticised by some feminists for the 'discipline' that comes to be exerted on women. For example, drawing on the ideas of Michel Foucault, both Sandra Bartky and Susan Bordo suggest that women's bodies are disciplined into taking on very particular and constrained shapes by the discourses of bodily perfectibility that is endemic to Western cultures (see pp. 107–8). Their work stresses how much effort and work on an ongoing daily basis it takes to 'produce' the normatively gendered, feminine body. Susan Bordo, in her study, particularly stresses the 'pathology' of the cultural expectation to be thin (Bordo 2003). Work on women's magazines has also, however, stressed the *pleasures* of feminine identifications.

Perhaps ironically, the idea that femininity needs work, that it is not a natural and inevitable part of being female, is an insight from women's magazine culture which is shared by feminists who utilise psychoanalysis, a very different perspective from that of the 'images of women' critique with which we started. These critics have made a profound intervention in debates about gender and the media. (For further investigation into the history of feminist film criticism see Thornham and Richardson 2013.)

Psychoanalysis in Feminist Media Studies: Women as Image

Many feminists are suspicious of psychoanalysis, the body of work associated with Sigmund Freud and others. Psychoanalysis suggests that much of what we think we know about ourselves is illusory because we are subject to unconscious processes of which we are only vaguely aware. At one time Freud's work was routinely dismissed by feminists as being complicit in the maintenance of patriarchal relations because his theories of infantile sexuality and the psychic processes that constitute identity are often read as if they are a blueprint for 'normal' (i.e. gender conformist and heterosexual) development. However, as has been widely noted by feminist media scholars, Juliet Mitchell (1975) challenged the assumption that the theory was recommending this, or that it was *proscriptive*. Rather, she argued that it was *descriptive*, an 'analysis' of *how* sexuality develops in a patriarchal society (ibid.: xiii; see also Rose 1983).

This unsettling of the very category of 'woman', assuming it not to be a pre-given certainty attained by all, was to become a key feature of queer theory's intervention in discussions about the subject of feminism (Butler 1990) and belongs, more broadly, to a post-structuralist account of subjectivity understood as precarious, unstable and fluid. Rose's work of this period (1986) stressed the significance for feminism of the work of French psychoanalyst Jacques Lacan's ideas about language. Lacan stressed that there are only two positions that it is possible to occupy within language: that of 'man' or 'woman'; and so language traps subjects into one of these. For the male child, under prevailing conditions, identity is in part achieved by his realisation that he has something girls don't have, thus he (unconsciously) assumes this must be the crucial thing. Masculinity is thus based on a fantasy of precarious wholeness which depends (for it to have meaning) on the fantasy of a lack in the 'other' (femininity). Masculine identity is then an achievement grounded in an identification with the phallus (a sign of power, associated with but not reducible to the male sexual organ). In this view, femininity then is also merely an achievement, or 'masquerade', certainly not an essence or reflection of an existing self, but, importantly, in this view it is a fantasy which emanates from the male position. At this point of course many feminists (and others) tend to throw their arms up in exasperation. However, as Sue Thornham points out (2000), Rose uses Lacan's work to stress the role of representation, fantasy and the unconscious in the production of sexed identity and its more general political and cultural repercussions, and which is of great interest to those working on media images. For media and film theory the insights of post-structuralism and psychoanalytic thinking on identity have emphasised how gendered meanings are established and maintained and how they operate on different levels.

In relation to film and media, psychoanalytic work stresses the uncovering of the unconscious processes at work in the very structures of cinema and its hold on the viewer. One aspect of this is the centrality of ideas of the cinematic gaze, which is described in Laura Mulvey's formidably influential article 'Visual Pleasure and Narrative Cinema' (1975), which can reasonably be said to have kept generations of media and film scholars arguing. Mulvey's article suggests that cinematic pleasure is the affirmation of the heterosexual fantasy of man as active, desiring subject and woman as passive, desired object. Mulvey argued that mainstream, narrative cinema is 'cut to the measure of male desire' leaving the spectator structurally locked into a preconstituted, gendered position through the three 'looks' (camera, character and director) that classical Hollywood cinema offers. Women, in this argument, are 'bearers' rather than 'makers' of meaning and the 'visual pleasure' of cinema is primarily a heterosexual male pleasure in looking *at* women. However, this pleasure, for men, is always highly ambivalent since it reminds them of the 'fact' of sexual difference, which is threatening. This threat, then, has to be contained. In cinema this containment happens through two narrative structures: the woman can be investigated and eventually punished for inspiring such castration anxiety; or, alternatively, this anxiety can be allayed through fetishisation of the female body (hair, legs, shoes, etc.). Where this structure leaves male desire *for*, as well as identification *with*, other men, and where it leaves the desiring *female* viewer, has subsequently been much debated (see pp. 35–40).

One area of debate has been in relation to femininity. Mary Anne Doane (1982), for example, suggested that the idea of a feminine masquerade (dependent as it is on a stress of the *performance* of femininity rather than as an essence) can enable a *distance* from the image and that stressing this gap enables a critical relation to the image, rather than the narcissism or masochism which Mulvey's account foregrounds. As Annette Kuhn points out, the possibilities opened up by the idea that femininity and masculinity should be understood as a process, rather than as an essence, takes on a more 'liberatory' agenda than Mulvey's initial paradigm suggested, in which spectators were locked into position (Kuhn 1994: 214–16). At best, as Kuhn points out, a psychoanalytically informed analysis combines both text and context, since it relates what is 'in the text' (the figure on the screen) to the operations of cinema itself (the apparatus) and where that places the viewer. However, it is open to the charge that it does not take the socially differentiated audience seriously, positing a monolithic or at least very limited range of possible subject positions for the female viewer (Gamman and Marshment, 1988) or indeed the male (Dyer 1982; Neale 1993), and doesn't take into account the ways that audiences are socially situated or indeed are invested in different ways in cinemagoing as an everyday practice and pleasure (Stacey 1994). Moreover, Mulvey's paradigm has been subject to very persuasive critiques from, amongst others, bell hooks and Lola Young who point out that the history of representing black women contrasts radically with that of white women. Black women's bodies are not idealised in the same way as white women's bodies and so 'looking relations' need to be understood within matrixes of power other than that of gender, where 'looking back' is a political act of resistance (hooks 1994: 207; Young 1996). Therefore, while psychoanalysis has offered key insights into the ways in which representations work at the level of structuring pleasure and desire according to the existing dynamics of (patriarchal) power, it is simultaneously open to the criticism that it is both exclusionary and universalising.

Popular Pleasures and Cultural Studies Perspectives

Mulvey's work had a radical agenda – to dismantle the prevailing forms of pleasure in order to create a different mode of not just viewing practice but of cinema itself. Her interest was precisely in creating alternative possibilities to mainstream or dominant representational practice. However, feminist media and cultural work influenced by psychoanalysis has not confined itself to an oppositional relationship to popular culture. On the contrary, feminist work on popular media has been characterised in part by an interrogation of feminine and female pleasure. Rosalind Coward's work, for instance, stressed the ambivalent and complex nature of the incitement of 'female desire' through popular forms such as the romance and popular music, which engage both conscious and unconscious processes with contradictory and ambivalent results in terms of women's pleasurable engagement with what look like very unprogressive texts. Other feminist work on popular genres such as soap opera made similar use of psychoanalysis to interrogate the pleasures for women of particular forms of narrative offered to them. Tania Modleski's work (1988), for example, stressed the specificity of female pleasures offered by romance and soap opera which have a feminine narrative structure which remains open and which also offer a range of points of identification and rejection.

The feminist media analyses that we have so far been discussing were predominantly interested in the text and its relation to the viewer, though not in how *particular* audiences consumed texts. However, audience consumption of texts did become an area of intense interest and some decisive debates over the meaning and significance of media texts in people's lives began to appear. Very different work on pleasure characterises the feminist work which was interested in the gender politics of popular culture genres, often understood as 'feminine'. The widespread denigration of much popular culture as trash and unworthy of serious academic interest was understood by many scholars as intensely problematic in its own right since for instance it confers 'cultural capital' on the middle class via their appreciation of 'serious' culture – part of a wider legitimation of class interests disguised as 'autonomous' aesthetic judgement. Whilst many cultural theorists of the left also denigrated mass culture, as (in an infamous phrase) 'pre-digested. It is baby-food' (Adorno 1991: 58), for feminist academics rather different questions were also in play. Importantly, there was a desire to account for the *pleasures* of popular culture for women. As already noted, some work in the psychoanalytic tradition was interested in gendered pleasures and desires. As Gill notes, this kind of work opened up new questions and understandings about the media beyond the 'images of women' critique; on the other hand, though, she suggests that much of the work that followed was overly reliant on 'textual determinism' and ran the risk of reproducing a kind of gender essentialism and 'lack of sensitivity to differences between women' (Gill 2007). Some of these problems were addressed through a greater emphasis on the role of the audience as creators and not just recipients of the text.

In part, the work Gill refers to as 'the turn to pleasure' was an attempt to get over the 'cultural dupe' thesis, which refers to the stress placed on the ideological function of media to maintain the status quo. These shifts are related to a wider debate within media, communication and cultural studies identified with the work of Stuart Hall and colleagues at the Birmingham Centre for Contemporary Cultural Studies. This wide ranging body of work challenged the existing approaches to audiences, which assumed a direct model of media influence over an audience, and argued for an approach which looked at media as part of a wider process of gaining 'consent'. They also challenged a view – often shorthanded to 'The Frankfurt School' – which stressed the manipulations of mass culture, characterised as a mass 'deception'. Many media and cultural scholars found highly unpalatable the passivity and the lack of agency attributed to the audience associated with such a view of media. In line with the broader emphasis on 'negotiation', and the use made of Gramsci's concept of 'hegemony', the work that comes under this rubric tried to account for why those benefiting least from existing inequalities (e.g. in terms of their class, race, gender or sexual positionality) did not actively seek 'liberation'. Hegemony emphasises power, though less as domination and more as the process of gaining and maintaining consent for the status quo which requires considerable maintenance and effort. As Ien Ang (1991) suggests, whilst in some ways cultural studies work on audiences might have similar research questions to those from other traditions, the differences are important. Cultural studies is avowedly political rather than distant and objective in that it assumes that there is a struggle and a negotiation to be made over the text and in the audience and, moreover, that there is not a scientific 'truth' to be found through audience research. Empirical study of the audience is understood as a vital component for understanding how media work and what the broader consequences are for thinking through questions of identity and politics.

Research Methods and Positions

For feminist scholars this interest in the audience turned out to be exceptionally fraught since what was at stake was not only a desire to understand the way that gendered ideologies gained 'consent' but that feminist research methods had also contested the position of 'outsider' and had emphasised the power relations inherent in research methodologies which took 'other women' as their subject. Questions are thus raised by feminists as to how necessary it is to reflect on one's own position in relation to the text and also the object of study – the audience and the female viewer in this case. In a discussion of the first 15 years of feminist television research, Charlotte Brunsdon (1997) refers to these debates as questions of identity for the critic and her 'other' the female viewer on whom she is reliant and whom she must 'produce' in her studies. Brunsdon notes that feminist research on 'women audiences' was part of a larger project for re-evaluating the cultural products and genres most associated with women. She notes too a general shift from text to audience 'across a range of social science and humanities disciplines' (ibid.: 115).

Brunsdon has three categories for the relationship between feminism/feminist critic and other women. First, the transparent 'we' – we women, which conceives all women as a 'sisterhood' – which Brunsdon conceives as a 'utopian, activist' moment historically defined in post-1960 feminism. This 'we' might be opposed to media depictions and as we have noted already this is open to the charge of political exclusions – which women? And on the basis of its epistemological assumptions, do women know differently? But this also opened the space for research to be imagined as a 'shared experience'.

Brunsdon's second category is the 'hegemonic' which references the 'recruitist' 'impulse to transform the feminine identifications of women to feminist ones' (ibid:118). Here, there was a separation made between the critic and the 'ordinary woman' with a feminist identity being constructed through the production of this difference (ibid.: 118). This position produced work on television (for example soap opera) which specifically distances itself from the object of study and from those who enjoy it. Brunsdon notes the difficulties for critics in occupying a variety of positions – the intellectual (traditionally non-gendered), the feminist (who wants to be 'we' women) and the disavowal of conventional femininity (the object under discussion – romance, soap opera).

The final position is 'fragmented' and characterised by a 'radical particularism' (ibid.: 120) and Brunsdon stresses the difficulty of seeing gender as the privileged or explanatory category for research projects which have the 'audience' as central. She notes that the theoretical assault on the category of 'woman' via postmodernism, post-structuralism and post-colonialism is one that is easier for women who are intellectual to inhabit. This typology is useful in that it delineates areas which another 15 years on are still pertinent to a consideration of the politics of feminist criticism.

These approaches to gender and media in relation to feminism all require us to think, as Rosalind Gill suggests (2007), about the role of the feminist critic. Should feminist critics be primarily concerned with recovering women's pleasure from dismissal? Or celebrating women's choices? Or concerned with ideological critique? Or looking for strands of resistance and subversion? The complexity of the issues raised so far in relation to gender in the media have stressed different approaches to media texts and their relation to spectators or audiences and how these are gendered and with what wider significances. A key strand of recent work on popular culture from a feminist perspective has been dominated by a particular term, 'post-feminism', a term which is notoriously difficult to define as it is often used in contradictory ways.

Post-feminism(s)

Post-feminism is a quite familiar but difficult and contested term used variously to refer to a range of ideas, from the description of a particular historical and cultural space and time to analysing changing gender roles. It describes, as we shall see in more detail in Chapter 4, a particular kind of engagement with *some* aspects of the feminist debates which we have been discussing in this chapter. Post-feminism has been described recently as a 'sensibility' (Gill 2007), a discursive construction (Projansky 2001) and as a 'set of assumptions' (Tasker and Negra 2007). The term is sometimes used in a positive way to note a shift in theorising gender following the insights of post-structuralism and critical race theory, or to highlight new plural identities and the possibilities for expanded understandings of agency (Genz and Brabon 2009). It is as often used in an almost diametrically opposed sense to describe the retrenchment of politically and culturally conservative positions in relation to gender, particularly as reflected in media representations.

In Anglo-American popular culture it is a term which has considerable currency and is often used as a shorthand for a particular kind of popular media figure (or, sometimes, student) – one who has gained from feminist politics and who sees absolutely no need for the grumpy, anachronistic and censorious feminist (Brunsdon 2006; McRobbie 2009) to carry on moaning about inequality whilst looking unkempt. This is a crude caricature of course, but it does hint at some of the particular features of post-feminist media culture (or discourse) which many commentators have noted. The key features of post-feminism, which a variety of critics have noted, are neatly summarised by Charlotte Brunsdon, who, while disliking the term, suggests that there is a consensus amongst critics that:

> its meanings have been contradictory, ranging from 'backlash' to new manifestations of feminism within popular culture; it entails different articulations of feminism and femininity; 'the girl' is its central figure; consumption is its core activity and irony a defining tone; there is a re-inscription of 'raunch' culture; its characteristic subjectivity is congruent with neoliberalism; it is a figure of privilege, associated particularly with white women in the US, and necessarily

with contexts in which 'feminism' had a second wave; it is often glossed with reference to fictional female characters in, for instance, Ally McBeal, Bridget Jones, and Sex and the City.

(Brunsdon 2013: 378)

In addition we should note that the term is very invested in women's appearance, often in relation to highly conventional forms of femininity which may be 'put on' and played about with, but which are surprisingly narrow; it is often exclusively heterosexual in its 'raunchy' 'sex positivity'.

A notable stress on consumer culture is one of the key features of post-feminism and has been crucial in relation to the various resignifications of domesticity and female labour and its relation to the 'home' (see Hollows 2006; Brunsdon 2006; Negra 2009). In their introduction to the revised version of the important anthology *Feminist Television Criticism*, published ten years after the original, the editors trace the legacy of the encounter between young privileged European and US women influenced by and drawn to second-wave feminism and their relation to domesticity and the housewife. This emphasis on the domestic is still very much in evidence in post-feminist culture where it has remained ambivalently central (as will be developed in Chapter 4). This has included a reclaiming of traditional feminine pursuits, but without the associations of subordination that early feminist critics like Betty Friedan had highlighted. So baking or knitting become recoded as leisure pursuits, often performed with an ironic flair (for example the growth of huge cupcake confections).

Tasker and Negra suggest that within popular discourses acknowledging feminism has 'frequently taken the form of a pre-packaged and highly commodifiable entity, so that discourses having to do with women's geographic, professional, and perhaps most particularly sexual freedom are effectively harnessed to individualism and consumerism' (Tasker and Negra 2005: 107). Post-feminism is not a straightforward backlash against feminism (although it contains elements of this); rather it is a highly contradictory set of discourses which operate as a 'double entanglement' with feminism (McRobbie 2009). On the one hand feminism is understood to have resolved 'old' problems of inequality between the sexes, for which post-feminism is grateful; on the other hand feminism is repudiated and disidentified with, often in the strongest terms.

Post-feminism, then, is a wide ranging discourse which cuts across media texts, in what Angela McRobbie memorably refers to as the 'aftermath of feminism' (McRobbie 2009) and which can be found in a diverse range of media including advertising and news as well as drama and film. It is characterised often by an apparent acceptance of some of feminism's critical positions. For example, Rosalind Gill demonstrates how advertising has successfully deflected feminist anger at the demeaning portrayal of women through an insistent use of 'irony' (Gill 2007) as an 'alibi' for what would otherwise be straightforward objectification. However, if feminism is an oppositional, political engagement with the world as it is, which it understands to be capable of transformation, post-feminism, on the other hand, seems to assume that gender is no longer a cause for examination. This, many critics argue, goes very much against the grain of the background of continuing inequality and gender hierarchy, and they note that this is where post-feminism is particularly, if quietly, coercive. As Angela McRobbie points out, post-feminism grants young women certain kinds of freedom, but at a price: 'the new female subject is, despite her freedom, called upon to be silent, to withhold critique, to count as a modern sophisticated girl, or indeed this withholding of critique is a condition of her freedom' (McRobbie 2007: 34). Critique, however, is the whole point of feminist engagement with media, and many see as much need for it now as ever.

This chapter has introduced some of the key ideas and debates that have structured feminist cultural theory and its critical application to the study of media images. We have seen how feminist politics has interrogated ideas of biological difference (sex) and cultural regimes of gender. The media is important in these debates because of the key role it plays in the formation, reproduction and (sometimes) contestation of hierarchically organised gender relations. The earliest form of feminist criticism challenged the (stereo) types of women deployed by the media, arguing that women were 'symbolically annihilated' (Tuchman et al.1978) by media representations which trivialised, erased and objectified women. Psychoanalytically informed work from the same period looked to the ways that sexual difference was implicated in structures of viewing (Mulvey 1975), whilst work from a cultural studies perspective sought to engage with some of the pleasures offered by engaging in feminine identifications (Stacey 1994) and female genres. Finally we considered the recent understanding of popular media as embedded in a post-feminist climate. Subsequent chapters will see how these insights can be applied to the critical study of contemporary media representations. In chapter 4 we will consider how some of these debates around femininity, pleasure, consumption, female roles and empowerment find their way into a particular form of media, the 'quality' television drama, where both within the texts themselves and in the surrounding media discourse these preoccupations are central. The intention here is to follow Kuhn's lead in providing gendered analysis and to thus 'make visible the invisible'.

2 Masculinities

The study of masculinities and the media comes from a very different political standpoint from the study of femininities, not least because, unlike femininity, masculinity has not required a political formation in order to advance its rights. As the last chapter has outlined, feminism has been interested in two main trajectories in the study of the representation of femininities in the media: images of women and women *as* images. 'Images of women' scholarship stems from a sociological imperative to explore the types of women that are represented in the media. What stereotypes are in place? Are women continually represented as either housewives/mothers or dutiful daughters or sex objects? And how can these representations function as a cultural barometer, commenting upon the politics of a specific culture or context? On the other hand, the scholarship on 'women as images' has addressed *how* women are represented on the screen with a particular focus on how the spectator views these images and the erotic dynamics of spectatorship. Key to the latter debates was Laura Mulvey's hugely influential essay 'Visual Pleasure and Narrative Cinema' which argued that, in mainstream narrative cinema, the woman's image on the screen connoted 'to-be-looked-at-ness'. In mainstream film, the woman functions as the object of the cinematic gaze. The viewing pleasure of mainstream narrative cinema is the reinforcement of the gendered binary of man as active desiring subject and woman as passive object. These starting points have elicited a wide range of scholarship on women, feminism and femininity in the media.

By contrast, the study of masculinities and the media does not arise from quite the same political starting point. Given that, until fairly recently, most mainstream cinema would represent a male protagonist, the hero of the narrative who fights through adversaries to win his prize (usually a beautiful woman), there seemed less necessity to examine how such an image could be deemed 'degrading' or 'offensive' to male spectators. Nonetheless scholarship in masculinity studies has attempted to deconstruct masculinity and make it visible. The project of masculinity studies has been to de-essentialise the role of men, as they are represented in media texts, exposing how these can be understood as re-presentations of a male-biased (patriarchal) culture. While 'images of women' scholarship explored how representations of women could promote greater feminine oppression, studies of 'images of men' have examined how men are represented in a privileged position and have attempt to denaturalise this position of power.

Masculinity is a precarious identification and, as such, is heavily guarded and policed by mainstream representations. In the Introduction we explained that, while sex is grounded in biology (male/female), gender (masculinity/femininity) is a cultural perform-ance (a learned pattern of behaviour) of this biological sex. The cultural role of masculinity as active and dominant (the male hero of narrative cinema) *cannot* be reduced to any single biological trait. There is noth-ing within the male body that asserts an essential activeness other than a cultural expectation of this role. Most importantly, these cultural expectations are supported, and reinforced, by media representations. Therefore, masculinity can be understood as a set of cultural perform-ances that men learn over time. Given the constructed nature of these performances, masculinity has always defined itself in terms of what it is not, and its main defining other has always been femininity.

From an early age, boys learn that performing femininity is one of the ultimate taboos for men and school playground bullying is very often structured around boys policing their masculinity by denigrating other boys who are deemed less masculine (see Parker 1996; Pascoe 2005). The target of schoolyard bullies will usually be boys who are, say, not good at sports or perhaps too fond of theatre or the performing arts. In other words, anything which is culturally identified as feminine is a risky pursuit for male bodies as it risks challenging the performance of masculinity. As such, misogyny (the fear of women) has often been a component of masculinity, given that masculinity must define itself against anything which is feminine, and one key strategy in defining self is to denigrate the performance of the binary opposite. If feminin-ity is belittled then masculinity is exalted. Indeed, many schoolyard fights (as one of the authors, a former teacher, can testify from experi-ence) are the result of boys trying to prove their masculinity by deni-grating any act of femininity that they find in their peers. Related to this, one of the ultimate transgressions in masculinity is when a man performs femininity – a fear which has been labelled 'effeminophobia' (Richardson 2003, 2009). When a man does femininity he is not only showing a respect for the defining other, against which masculinity identifies itself, but he is demonstrating that gender *is* a cultural performance. A male body can do femininity, just as a female body can perform masculinity (see Halberstam 1998). The effeminate male body demonstrates that masculinity is merely an act – a set of culturally learned performances – and therefore deconstructs the very identity that is so precious to male bodies.

Therefore, masculinity is a very unstable identification. If the fantasy of masculinity as active and dominant is to be maintained, then the illusion of masculinity as a fixed, essential property of male bodies also needs to be supported. The political agenda of masculinity studies has been to deconstruct masculinity, showing that it is *not* essential but rather a cultural performance. As such, in recent years masculinity has continually reinvented itself, responding to the political imperative of the time. Much media criticism (the 'images of men' debates) has considered how different masculine identifications have emerged over the past few decades as a result of the articulation of feminism, gay liberation and queer politics. In the second half of this chapter we will consider these debates, focusing on the cultural politics of 1980s 'new masculinity' through to the 1990s 'new laddism' and finally reflecting on the identification of 'metrosexuality'.

However, in the first section we will look at the 'men as images' debates and consider the dynamics of gendered spectatorship. If the representation of the female body in mainstream art/media connotes 'to-be-looked-at-ness' (Mulvey 1975), and reinforces the patriarchal belief in man as active desiring subject and woman as passive object, then how are male bodies represented? How can the male body bear the objectification of the camera's gaze in both still and moving images while still conveying the sense of masculine empowerment – the patriarchal necessity of man as active desiring subject? Hence in the first section we explore the dynamics of gazing upon male bodies in the media – *how* men are represented – while in the second section we will consider what types of masculinity are being represented and how masculine identifications have had to modify as a result of changes in cultural politics.

Gazing upon the Male Body

In his hugely influential book on the representation of gender in art, John Berger established a paradigm which has been central to the study of gender in visual culture. According to Berger, throughout the history of Western art, there is a gendered binary to be found in the representation of bodies and in the act of looking at these representations: 'Men act and women appear. Men look at women. Women watch themselves being looked at' (Berger 1972: 64). This is most obvious in the history of the representation of the nude in art. A female nude is relaxed – a body in repose, inviting the gaze of the spectator to marvel at her beauty. One particular motif, popular in the representation of the female nude, is the mirror in which the female nude gazes upon her own beauty. The result of the naturalisation of this image is to make the female body complicit in the act of objectification and to underscore the similarity in the ways women and men view the female body, as passively surveyed through the male perspective. By contrast, the male body was usually (but not always – there are some notable exceptions which will be considered later) a body in action. The fact that the male body was also in various stages of undress (and warriors were usually featured in this way) was more a testament to the power and strength of the male body, rather than a reflection on the beauty of that body. An old art history joke is: 'When is a nude not a nude? When it's male'. It does indeed seem to be the case that when a female body is without clothes it assumes the role of the eroticised nude, while a male body simply appears undressed. Revealing the masculine physique is a signifier of strength and power rather than passivity and objectification. We have only to think of the very masculine act of a man removing his shirt in public – an activity common with men who are engaged in laborious or strenuous work, such as builders or workmen. The same activity could never be the case for women, as a woman removing her shirt in public would have a very different connotation.

The theorist to develop Berger's arguments in relation to contemporary media has been Richard Dyer who published a very influential article entitled 'Don't Look Now' (1982) in which he analysed the ways in which the male body is represented in contemporary, still images. The key problem with representing the male body – especially within a genre such as the 'pin up photograph' – is that this act of objectification can reduce the male to a passive body (what Mulvey calls 'to-be-looked-at-ness') rather than to an active subject. Dyer argues that there are various strategies at work in contemporary representations which maintain the illusion of power and activity, even if the body is represented in repose. First, Dyer points out that the male body, if undressed, will always tauten and flex its muscles, thus suggesting that even though the body is temporarily in repose it is ready for action at any moment. Muscularity is (wrongly) assumed to be a natural, biological signifier of maleness. However, as we explained in the Introduction, this belief is simply another example of a cultural performance which is believed to be essential as muscularity does not just *happen* to any body – male or female – but is the product of sustained work, including hours spent in the gym and adherence to a specific dietary regime (see Locks and Richardson 2010). For this reason, many feminists lauded the activity of female bodybuilding which was not only a rejection of traditional, feminine iconography but denaturalised the assumption of muscles as a natural male attribute (Guthrie and Castelnuovo 1992; St Martin and Gavey 1996; Coles 1999; Richardson 2008a). Nevertheless, Dyer is correct to point out that muscularity is the *assumed* signifier of male power and strength, and so if the representation draws attention to the male model's muscularity it reminds the spectator of the belief in masculinity as *essentially* active despite the fact that the body is represented in a state of repose. The point is that even though the body may not be active at the minute, it looks as if it's always ready for action. This belief in muscularity as the essential attribute of men, and the signifier of 'natural' male strength, certainly helps to explain the pleasure that watching a bodybuilding competition may give its spectators. It does not matter if the huge muscles on stage are technically unable to lift heavy weights – the key point is that they look as if they can (see Locks and Richardson 2011).

Second, Dyer points out that a key element in the iconography of representing still images of men is the gaze of the male model himself. Dyer explains that the male model often elevates his gaze as if suggesting that, firstly, he is utterly indifferent to the fact that spectators are gazing upon him and, secondly, implying that his mind is on higher things than the trivial, irrelevant act of being objectified by the camera. Most importantly this uplifted gaze suggests that the male model is unaware of the beauty of his body. Unlike female models, the men are not complicit in the act of objectification (there are *very* few images of men gazing upon their own reflection in a mirror) and instead the representation implies that they are simply using their bodies to get a specific job done – whether this be manual labour or valiant warfare. Indeed, historically there has been a gendered distinction between the head and the body in which the head/intellect has been deemed masculine while the body has been deemed feminine (see Spelman 1982). In this respect, the male model's elevated gaze, suggesting that his mind is on higher things, is not only his disregard for the trivial gaze of the camera but a reaffirmation of the connection between masculinity and the intellect. Even though the male model is being represented because of his 'beautiful' body, the act of the elevated gaze reinforces the belief in the intellect as a masculine preserve.

Dyer points out that the other alternative gaze of the model is that he returns the gaze of the camera in a confrontational fashion. While female models often lower their eyes, unable to respond to the investigative gaze of the camera's lens, the male model often stares coolly – even confrontationally – at the viewer, almost challenging the spectator to reduce him to the status of object. In this respect the model suggests that if he is being objectified it is with his consent and he is very aware of the mechanism at work within the photographic gaze. Certainly there are very few images in which the male body appears to have been caught off guard – as is very common for female bodies, especially in fashion photography. Various critics have developed Dyer's writing, in particular Susan Bordo (1999) and Kenneth MacKinnon (1997), who have explored the representation of the male body in the media and popular culture.

Dyer's article considered the codes of representing the male body as a pin-up – a still image in which the male body is offered as an object for the spectator's gaze. His thesis analysed how the male body can still suggest activity and dominance *despite* being positioned as an object. However, what about the representation of the male body within moving images – especially mainstream narrative cinema? If, as Mulvey argues, the female body in cinema connotes 'to-be-looked-at-ness' then what happens to the male body when it is represented on the screen? Two very influential critics who took up these debates, and reconsidered the Mulveyan formula, are Steve Neale and Paul Willemen.

According to the Mulveyian formula, the male spectator complies with the cinematic gaze which objectifies the female body. By contrast, the male body on the cinema screen is, arguably, not a source of erotic contemplation but a body with which the male spectator identifies. This formula has been cited as problematic for a number of reasons. Firstly, it ignores the question of the female spectator, and in that respect it overlooks specific genres which have been identified as 'women's films' (see p. 73). Neale points out that in genres such as the melodrama and the musical, the Mulveyan formula is problematic. Neale uses the example of the film musical *Saturday Night Fever* in which John Travolta's body – especially the sequence in which he engages in beautifying his body in preparation for a night of dancing – is very much a scene in which this body is objectified and offered to the spectator for erotic pleasure. Similarly, many melodramas objectify the male body and Neale cites an early example in the representation of Rock

Hudson's body in the 1950s melodramas of Douglas Sirk (see also Meyer 1991). Unlike other male stars, Hudson's body seems to yield to the camera, offering itself to the spectator as a source of erotic pleasure.

However, even if we assume that the spectator is male and heterosexual, there are problems with the Mulveyan paradigm of positing the male hero only as a source of identification. First, identification is not necessarily distinct from desire. This has particular relevance for same-sex sexual attraction (gay male sexuality) where the element of narcissistic identification may, obviously, play an element in the dynamics of desire. Second, and more importantly for film criticism, do the dynamics of cinema spectatorship prevent the male body being the object of the gaze? Both Neale and Willemen argue that the male body can indeed be the object of the gaze but that, unlike the female body, the male must not be *explicitly* represented as such. Instead, the male body must be represented in a state of activity thus suggesting that this body is not simply being placed on display, as an object for the erotic delight of the spectator, but is a testament to the power and dominance of masculinity. This is most obvious in the genre known as the (Hollywood) action movie in which the male body is often exposed – shirts are ripped off as bodies fight and grapple with other bodies and/or aliens and monsters – though the revelation of this body is in order to suggest its power and strength rather than to exploit its erotic potential. Even in sequences where the male body appears to be in repose, there is always the *implication* that this body is not simply offered to the spectator but that it is a suggestion of the suppressed power of that body. For example, the start of the action film *The Terminator* reveals Schwarzenegger's nude body because he will soon be smashing up a few other bodies in the next scene.

Nevertheless, although the revelation of the male body on screen is always veiled by the agenda of demonstrating power and activity, the question of (homo) eroticism cannot be so easily dismissed. As long as the body is both the focus and agent of sexual desire, then the question of eroticism cannot be overlooked when this body is represented. Indeed, Paul Willemen famously argued that the look of the spectator at the male body may not merely be a mediation in order to attain the look at the female body, through identification with the gaze of the male protagonist, but that the look at the male body may be a source of pleasure in itself. In this respect, there is always an unquiet pleasure in gazing upon the male body as it may tap into what Willemen terms 'repressed homosexual looking' (1981). The spectator may well gain a considerable amount of (erotic) pleasure from watching the male body move, perform tasks or fight with other bodies. However, given that homoerotic looking is not sanctioned by hetero-masculinity, this erotic look at the male body must be 'paid for'. Therefore, Willemen argues that this is one of the reasons why the male action hero's body is brutalised and sadistically punished throughout the course of the narrative. In every action film, the hero must be bruised, beaten and nearly pummelled to death before rising victorious at the end. This is not simply a narrative convention but a way of ensuring that the spectator 'pays' for the guilty pleasure of the homoerotic gaze at the male body.

One film which makes a very deliberate comment about this dynamic is the highly self-reflexive *Fight Club* – a film which, arguably, has done more to deconstruct masculinity than any other cultural text. Set in the world of an illegal, underground fight club, the film has been considered a key text in the documentation of how contemporary masculinity is 'in crisis'. The uneasy pleasure of *Fight Club* is the way it vacillates so deliberately between the glorification of male activity/fighting and homoerotic spectatorship. Yet the payment for this uneasy pleasure is one of the most brutal in the history of cinema as the hero pulverises the face of a very pretty, young member of the fight club who is known as 'Angel Face'. As the hero smashes the man's face into a pulp, this is not only a demonstration of the character's rage and (sexual) frustration but is the masochistic payment the spectator must endure for the homoerotic spectatorship of the previous sequences. Of course, after the beating, Angel Face's beauty is now destroyed and so the source of the disquieting homoeroticism has been annihilated. Yet what makes *Fight Club* such a disconcerting experience is that the film draws attention to this mechanism (even the character's name, Angel Face, is far from subtle), forcing the male spectator to acknowledge how this dynamic is also at work in every mainstream action film. Probably more than any other contemporary Hollywood film, *Fight Club* exposes the uncertainties and insecurities of masculinity and reveals a gender which is, very much, in crisis.

Therefore in the next section we will consider the analyses of 'images of men', engaging with film/media texts as cultural barometers and considering how these popular cultural representations comment upon the gender politics of the particular period.

Images of Men

To emphasise once again, the analyses of representations of masculinity in popular media comes from a very different political trajectory from analysing images of women. Indeed, until the intervention of feminism, men had the luxury of considering themselves as not even being gendered, in the same way that white people have had (until recently) the luxury of not considering themselves as raced. Masculinity was simply a 'given' and certainly nothing to be debated or analysed.

However, the rise of second-wave feminism led to the realisation of how gender differs from sex. To repeat, while sex is grounded in biology (male and female), gender (masculine and feminine) is a cultural performance of various roles attributed to the body's sex. Therefore, while a body's sex – male and female – is universal, what is identified as masculine or feminine is a matter of culture and can change according to location or historical context. What was deemed an appropriate or fashionable performance of masculinity in Renaissance England would have been very different from the performance required by contemporary culture. It was one of the key agendas of second-wave feminism to denaturalise gender, to argue that femininity and masculinity should not be reduced to biology. On a very basic level, why is masculinity synonymous with activity and femininity with passivity? There is nothing inherent or essential in either the male or female body which makes this the case.

Given the open articulation of second-wave feminism, masculinity in the late 1980s was said to have entered a period of crisis. Arguably masculinity has always been in crisis and there have been various moments of upheaval throughout the 20th century. For example, the years after World War Two saw a big shake-up in gender roles as women were unwilling to relinquish the 'masculine' jobs they had held during the war. However, we generally refer to the period after the open articulation of second-wave feminist politics as the period in which masculinity was *really* in crisis.

Western media (in particular Hollywood cinema) can be seen to document this cultural shift in its representations. The action cinema, in particular, responded to the crisis of masculinity – and the 1980s became dominated by a genre which is commonly referred to as the 'hard bodies cinema' (see Tasker 1993; Jeffords 1994). Action stars such as Schwarzenegger, Stallone and Van Damme dominated the box office with film performances which revelled in their muscular masculinity and the feats which their bodies could perform. In many ways, these texts can be read as an attempt to soothe masculine anxieties in a period of masculinity in crisis. In other words, if feminism deconstructed masculinity (showing that masculinity was simply a performance, something the body does and not its essential or inherent property) then a film which exalts physical strength and muscularity (the *assumed* essential attribute of male bodies) can be seen to reaffirm essentialist notions of masculine power. In all the action films, it is the hero's physical strength which wins the day and saves everyone from the villain or monster. One possible reading of these films is that masculine strength – the *assumed* natural, essential preserve of male bodies – is what provides victory for the hero and thus asserts the belief that masculinity is the 'dominant' gender.

However, towards the end of the 1980s there was a more sensitive response to the articulation of second-wave feminist politics in the form of what is now termed 'new masculinity'. The 'new man' was an insightful response to the activism of feminist politics and represented a form of masculinity which was aware of its performances – most importantly how they could offend or oppress others – and instead offered a response to the politics of feminism. Instead of arrogant machismo, new man offered an iconography which was still traditionally masculine but with a much softer side (see Mort 1988; Nixon 2001). It was this mixture of hard and soft which distinguished new man from earlier representations. In other words, new man maintained a performance of hard masculinity, but with an awareness that this was merely a performance and which was able to incorporate softer elements into the image. Most importantly, new man imagery was distinguished from earlier popular cultural representations by a more openly sexualised representation of the male body which often drew upon codes which had previously only been employed for the female body. One of the iconic images of 'new masculinity' was the *L'Enfant* photo – a poster which would grace the walls of countless university student dorms in the late 1980s /early 1990s. This image featured a hard bodied, traditionally handsome male model but represented him cradling a tiny baby in his arms. The image suggested two things: firstly the man was responding sensitively to the politics of feminism and offering a softer, more sensitive, image – holding the baby and therefore sharing parental duties rather than conforming to archaic, essentialist ideas of the wife/mother as the essential parental guardian. Secondly, the image is an undeniably sensual icon in which the male body is erotically coded and offered to the spectator's gaze. Cinema too would respond to new man iconography, out of which the 'hard bodies' genre could be seen to evolve – most notably in the career of Arnold Schwarzenegger. This more sensitive new man – a body which combined traditional masculine hardness with performances previously identified as feminine – could be seen in the transformation of the sci-fi character 'The

Terminator', who was revised for the 1991 sequel *Terminator 2*. A similar new man role appeared in Schwarzenegger's later film *Kindergarten Cop* where the hard-bodied police officer became a successful kindergarten teacher. In *Kindergarten Cop*, Schwarzenegger's bulging biceps were not only used to fight the bad guys but to hold a children's novel which he read to the schoolchildren at story time.

The mid-1990s, however, saw a backlash against the politics of the 'feminised' new man as 'new lad' signalled a return to pre-feminist sexism, machismo and downright disrespectful behaviour. The term 'new lad' is synonymous with the British magazine *Loaded*: a magazine which is irreverent, vulgar and combines elements of top-shelf soft porn publications with a puerile interest in the scatological and disgusting. Imelda Whelehan succinctly describes 'new lad' culture as 'a renaissance of Benny Hill style "naughtiness" and "schoolboy vulgarity"' (Whelehan 2000: 65–6). As Bethan Benwell argued, the 'new lad' was not only reacting against feminism but also against 'middle-class culture' (2004: 6). Indeed, a great deal of new lad iconography is the emulation of working-class signifiers even if the subject is himself middle class. (In London culture the emulation of a fake Cockney accent – known as 'mockney' – is a key component in new lad identifications.) Partly this emulation of working-class signifiers is a reaction against the middle-class-based agenda of 'gender politics'. One particular criticism of feminism has always been that it addresses the concerns of middle-class, educated, Western, white women. Debating gender inequality is the luxury of people enjoying middle-class capitalism. Others, who are less privileged, may simply be struggling to find enough money for food or basic human necessities and are therefore unable to engage with feminist politics. Working-class culture has historically been more concerned with day-to-day maintenance than speculating on the politics of gender inequality.

However, new lad's rejection of middle-class sensibilities may also be inspired by the articulation of gay liberation politics and the ever increasing presence of gay men in metropolitan settings. One of the interesting aspects of gay identification within British Culture is the connection it has always held to middle-class culture. The cultural historian who has meticulously traced this has been Alan Sinfield who, in his case study of Oscar Wilde (1994), discovered that it was because of Wilde's sensationalised public disgrace and downfall that male middle-class sensibilities became coded in the public eye as synonymous with homosexuality. Wilde was very much a dandy – a figure of upper-middle-class, masculine laxity – and behaved in a fashion which we would now identify as effeminate. However, before Wilde's public disgrace this dandiness – attention to clothes, grooming, beautifying of the self – was not considered indicative of homosexuality but simply of middle-class laxity. After Wilde's downfall, however, the Wildean persona became *the* signifier of homosexuality and so male middle-class sensibility – performing the role of the dandy – became tarnished with the brush of homosexuality. In this respect, there has always been a link between male middle-class performance and the connotation of homosexuality. Working-class men, by contrast, have never been considered in the same way. 'Gay' became a middle-class identification and something which was not (readily) available to working-class men. In this respect, new lad iconography can be seen as reacting not only to feminism but to middle-class culture and implicitly to the rise of gay liberation politics.

Most importantly, new lad culture is, it has been widely noted, always cloaked with a veil of postmodern irony (Whelehan 2000; Gill 2007). The subtitle of *Loaded* magazine is 'for men who *should* know better', thus suggesting that men engaging in 'new laddist' behaviour should know how offensive it may be to women (and, arguably, also to gay men) but yet who continue to do so because they're not being very serious about it. One particular representational strategy employed in *Loaded*'s discourse is to make a particularly offensive comment and then follow it with a 'just kidding', thus suggesting that everything articulated within the discourse is 'ironic'.

Mainstream media and film came to adopt the paradigms of the new lad in the British sitcom *Men Behaving Badly*; and Hollywood also came to feature new lad ideology in various gross-out comedies, especially in the *American Pie* series of films. More recently these films have been joined by a series of what Hansen-Miller and Gill call 'Lad Flicks' which 'combine different genre elements to focus specifically on the interpersonal difficulties facing contemporary masculinity ... the humor of these films derives from what they depict as the juvenile nature of culturally identifiable masculine values and ideals' (2011: 40–1). These films (e.g. *The 40 Year Old Virgin, Knocked Up, Forgetting Sarah Marshall*, to name a few), they argue, revolve around the maturation of the male leads defined through the assumption of heterosexual domestic responsibilities and the rejection of the 'immature' male group. These films 'offer up a depiction of masculinity as fallible, damaged and distinctly un-heroic' (ibid.: 42). While they may play on earlier generic 'buddy film' traits which ward off the ever present 'threat' of the intensity of the male bonds being read as gay (through humour, aggressive disavowal, etc.), these films also utilise the irony card to particular effect regarding homophobic remarks: 'the "irony" derives from the manner in which such jokes are seemingly less direct attacks upon an existent sexual minority than they are self-deprecating jokes about the homosexual potentials of heterosexual men. In this way lad flicks acknowledge the idea that men who are homophobic habor unconscious fears about being gay, while nonetheless leaving the denigrated status of homosexuality completely intact' (ibid.: 45).

The late 1990s /early 2000s also saw the birth of another cultural trend in masculine identification: the 'metrosexual'. If 'new lad' reacted against 'new man', then the 'metrosexual' responded to new lad culture. The term itself was (arguably) coined by the journalist Mark Simpson and aims to describe a type of man who is driven by consumerism, fashion and a meticulous care of self. The 'metrosexual' is the man who moisturises (after cleansing and toning, of course) and invests his leisure time in consumerism and caring for his body (gym membership is essential). Although, on a superficial level, the metrosexual holds similarities with the ideologies of new man, it is important to remember that both identifications come from very different political and historical contexts. Separated by almost a decade, the identifications of 'new man' and 'metrosexual' are also the result of very different cultural politics. While new man was a sensitive response to the articulations of second-wave feminism, metrosexuality is a more sympathetic response to the open articulation of metropolitan gay culture. The metrosexual lifestyle is based upon the iconography and practices of metropolitan gay men: shopping, care of self and gym culture. As the 1990s saw the development of highly visible gay culture in major metropolitan cities (especially New York and London), gay male fashion started to influence all aspects of urban culture. It has often been speculated that metropolitan gay men have above-average spending power (the argument lies in the fact that, until recently, gay men would not have had children and so would have higher than average disposable incomes) and that they can invest their surplus money in consumer practices and care of the self. Arguably, a great deal of gay iconography (especially the image of being well groomed with well-developed muscularity) is attractive to *all* men (gay and straight) – and so many metropolitan gay men have aimed to attain this identification. The point is that although 'new masculinity' and 'metrosexuality' may offer similar iconography, they are inspired by different cultural politics.

The media was particular influential in shaping metrosexual identification, not least through its 'mainstreaming' of gayness in its dramas and television shows. As various critics have argued, television dramas such as *Sex and the City*, although featuring four female leads, can be read as an allegory of metropolitan gay lifestyle (Merck 2004; see also pp. 70–2), while other television shows have represented gay lifestyle as not only chic but also suggesting that gay men 'do everything better' than their straight counterparts. The very successful sitcom *Will and Grace* followed the room-mate relationship between a straight woman (Grace) and a gay man (Will). Not only was Will represented as a much more 'decent' person than the majority of straight men whom Grace encountered but he was also shown to function as more of a guardian figure to Grace, exceeding the requirements of friend/room-mate. Grace was usually shown to be utterly incompetent at most activities and it was usually Will who had to step in to save situations and pick up the pieces. Therefore, the show offered a representation of gay male sexuality in which the gay man was represented in a more favourable light than either the straight female lead or the straight male characters. This heroicising of a gay male character was something unprecedented in media representations (see Richardson et al. 2013).

However, where the agenda of metrosexualisation was really emphasised was in one of the most popular genres in contemporary media: the make-over show. In Chapter 5 we consider the dynamics of the make-over show in more detail but at this point it is important to stress that these shows were usually explicitly gendered in that the body which was 'made-over' (or transformed) was usually female. The year 2003 saw the birth of a highly popular new make-over show (originally an American show but a format which was later adopted by British television) entitled *Queer Eye for the Straight Guy*. The premise of the show was quite simple: a team of make-over experts would transform a slightly slobby, down-at-heels, heterosexual man. (Very often this man performed the iconography associated with new lad until the 'queer eyes' transformed him.) Each member of the 'queer eye' make-over team had a 'specialism' which ranged from teaching cookery skills to giving advice on grooming and care of self. The newly made-over subject would then demonstrate the success of his newly groomed, more sophisticated self by going on a date with his girlfriend/wife, while the five make-over experts watched him on camera. The novel twist of the show was that the five make-over experts were all gay men and identified themselves with the team label 'the fab five'.

On one level, this make-over show was simply emphasising a class-biased aesthetic in which middle-class decorum was being celebrated. If new lad celebrated a performed (ironic) working-class sensibility then metrosexuality lauded middle-class affluence. The make-over subject was always ungroomed and slobby but the team insisted upon the importance of middle-class taste and decorum; a change which was then heartily approved of by the man's girlfriend and colleagues. Yet the show also did something very unusual in its format by having gay men make over a heterosexual man. As we've already argued, this mapped neatly on to the elevation of gay male sensibility – gay men as harbingers of style and good taste – corresponding to the representation found in other contemporary shows such as *Will and Grace*. However, as Dennis Allen (2006) points out, the fact that the five make-over specialists were identified as gay doesn't really seem to impact upon the *type* of skills which they imparted to the make-over subject. They didn't, for example, make the man engage in metropolitan gay pursuits such as going to a gym. Yet what the show did, in its very format, was force the heterosexual male subject to inhabit a position which is normally the preserve of gay men in that he was placed simultaneously within the position of desiring subject *and* desired object. This was made particularly clear in the final sequence in which the newly made-over man went on a date with his girlfriend – often this was a date in his flat so that he could demonstrate his newly gained culinary talents and show off his immaculately styled home. In this respect, the man was in the traditionally active role of 'courting' his girlfriend and trying to impress her with his acts of contemporary chivalry. However, while performing these actions he was observed by the fab five, and the show's spectators, who gazed upon his actions while he showered, shaved and prepared himself for the date. In this respect the man was made acutely aware of his role as both active seducer but also as desired object (the fab five never missed an opportunity to make risqué comments about the man's body as he showered and shaved) and, as such, he was placed in a position which is normally only held by gay men. As Dennis Allen argues, 'on *Queer Eye* the straight man is repositioned into an osmotic perception of the self as both desiring subject and desired object that has historically been considered the province of women and gay men' (ibid.: 6). Metrosexuality, therefore, is not simply a revision of new man ideology but is a sympathetic response to gay culture in which straight men not only appropriate elements of gay iconography and style but also voluntarily place themselves in the position of both active desiring subject and desired object.

In this chapter we have attempted to overview the debates relevant to the study of masculinities in the popular media. We have outlined the dynamics of *how* we look at the male body in representation and have considered how the media has represented contemporary masculine identifications from the 1980s to the present day. In the next chapter, we consider the possibility of moving beyond the gender binary, challenging the very relevance of that binary system itself, as we investigate the intriguing debates found within queer theory.

3 Beyond the Two-Gender System: Queer Theory

In the previous two chapters we have considered masculinity and femininity as a fixed binary system. Both masculinity and femininity operate for defining other people, and the various cultural institutions – family, school, media – police bodies into one category or the other. Criss-crossing between masculinity and femininity, or performing within a space between the two identifications, is culturally frowned upon, and people who do so may risk being socially ostracised or labelled 'queer'. In this chapter we consider these issues by introducing you to the debates within contemporary queer theory.

At this point, it is worth emphasising that the identification of 'queer' is used in a variety of different ways by different political groups. Some people simply use 'queer' as a synonym for lesbian and gay. 'Queer' can indeed function as a useful shorthand – a convenient umbrella term – for all sexual minorities: lesbian, gay, bisexual. However, in the context of gender studies we argue that 'queer' is not simply a synonym for lesbian or gay. 'Queer' stems from the Latin verb *torquere* (to twist) and literally means 'unusual' or 'strange'. As Michael Warner famously argued, 'queer' defines itself against regimes of the normal rather than heterosexuality (1993: xxvi). In this respect, it is problematic to consider 'queer' as a synonym for gay or lesbian given that there are many gays and lesbians who are perfectly happy with 'normal' and do not see themselves as any different from the rest of society other than in their choice of sexual object. Therefore, it is fair to assert that 'queer' is a distinctly political identification rather than simply one describing an erotic preference (Bersani 1995: 2). Most importantly, 'queer' is not simply to be reduced to the agenda of choice of sexual object in which it is taken to describe mismatches or incoherencies in the assumed stable continuum of sex, gender and sexuality. For example, a body which is sexed as female but is doing masculinity may be identified as a queer subject – irrespective of whether this body identifies as heterosexual. Likewise, a male and female couple who engage in 'unconventional' sex acts can be identified as queer even though they are a heterosexual couple. Certainly (hetero) sexual activity is taking place between this couple but this unconventional act is queering the assumed gender roles of active and passive. In other words, 'queer' is used to describe anything which challenges or disrupts traditional or hegemonic regimes of gender, sexuality and sexual desire.

Arguably, the founder of queer theory is the philosopher Judith Butler who, in 1990, published a hugely influential book entitled *Gender Trouble*. Although Butler wrote the book with a feminist agenda, the particular debates that she raised in the text are now regarded as the foundation stones of contemporary queer theory. Butler argued that feminism had failed to achieve its goals. Both first and second-wave feminism had simply locked bodies into the limiting, hierarchical binary of masculine/feminine. Although second-wave feminism had demonstrated that masculinity and femininity were cultural constructs, neither category was being challenged or overthrown when they remained in their simplistic, binary system. Therefore, Butler called for a gender politics which would see gender as a more fluid variable which was not limited to having to slot into this binary system.

Central to Butler's argument was her adoption of the linguistic term 'performative'. This term was made famous by the linguist John Austin who argued that language could be divided into two areas: constative and performative. Constative language is merely descriptive and, as such, constitutes the majority of utterances. Examples of constative expressions might be: 'It's a rainy day' or 'That is a blue shirt'. In other words, constative language simple describes what is there. Performative utterances are different in that they are expressions which change the status of the subject they are referring to. The most commonly cited example of a performative utterance is the marriage ceremony where the priest or vicar pronounces the man and woman in front of him to be husband and wife. 'I now pronounce you husband and wife' is not a constative utterance but a performative utterance in that this phrase has changed the status of the man and woman in the church. They are no longer simply a man and a woman; now they are husband and wife. Examples of other performative utterances include 'You are under arrest' and 'I bet £1,000 on that roll of the dice'. In other words, performative utterances are expressions which change the cultural status of the subject. However, it is important to remember that, unlike constative utterances, performatives require the subject to be recognised within a specific social matrix. For example, it is only the priest/vicar/registrar who can pronounce the man and woman to be husband and wife. If an 'unqualified' person (a man on the street) were to pronounce them to be that, the utterance would be meaningless. As such, performative utterances/gestures are only intelligible (i) within a specific social structure which bestows authority on the person making the utterance and (ii) when that person understands the technicalities of the utterance. (The pronouncement of 'husband and wife' is only intelligible if it takes place in a culture which acknowledges traditional matrimony.) Therefore, performative utterances always require witnesses – people who can confirm and validate that the expression has legitimacy within this specific culture. Again, the marriage ceremony makes this obvious by demanding actual witnesses who will sign the register and confirm that the performative pronouncement of marriage has taken place.

Butler famously reworked this concept of performativity in relation to gender. In a much quoted passage, she argued that 'there is no gender identity behind the expressions of gender; that identity is performatively constituted by the very "expressions" that are said to be its results' (1990: 33). Although second-wave feminism had argued that gender was not essential, but instead was something which the body did, Butler's paradigm of performativity gave us a specific and succinct way of interpreting this 'doing' by identifying it as a performative effect. Instead of arguing, for example, that we have a female body which is then doing femininity, Butler turned the equation on its head and argued that there are doings and expressions of femininity which a body does and which performatively constitute the identification of 'feminine'. Here, Butler was reworking the philosophy of Friedrich Nietzsche (1996 [1887]: 29) in relation to gender. If Nietzsche argued that there is no being who precedes the deed as 'the doer' – it is merely a fiction imposed on the doing; the doing itself is everything, then Butler argued that our gender identification functions in the same way.

However, many people misread Butler's thesis and confused performativity with performance. Performance is voluntary and is utilised at will. The actor is on the stage performing the Shakespearian character Hamlet but, when he leaves the stage, he stops performing that role. Butler makes it clear that although gender is not natural, neither is it simply a performance which can be shrugged on and off at will. The body does not simply go to the wardrobe in the morning and pick out a gender for the day (Butler 1993: x). Performativity, unlike voluntary performance, is implicated in social and cultural regimes which, like the marriage ceremony, is dependent upon validation from witnesses and specific social structures/rules which authenticate this performative gesture. In that respect, the very first performative utterance, which a body is ever likely to encounter, is at birth when the gynaecologist proclaims 'It's a boy!'. This is not only a performative utterance but a type of threat for the subject. Implicit in this statement is the warning that the body should do boyishness/masculinity for the rest of its life. If the body violates the performative utterance 'It's a boy!' then that body risks becoming an unintelligible subject; a queer subject.

Queer theory, however, does not stop at considering the importance of gender performativity in relation to gender politics but moves the discussion towards considerations of how this relates to sexuality. The term 'heterosexuality' can be broken into two words ('hetero' and 'sexuality') and means the sexualisation of difference ('hetero' = 'difference'). In other words, hetero-sexuality is the eroticisation of difference while homo-sexuality ('homo' = 'same') is the eroticisation of sameness. The 'difference' that is eroticised is not (for the most part) class or race but gender. It is gender which is the scaffold for eroticism. Masculinity sparks off its opposite – femininity – and creates the erotic frisson. Aretha Franklin sings 'you make me feel like a natural woman' because the man she is with is doing traditional, or hegemonic, masculinity and this sparks off against her femininity and feels right or, as she calls it, 'natural'. However, what is actually being eroticised in the lyrics 'you make me feel like a natural woman'? What the singer is praising is the gender of the love object – the masculinity. However, as Butler has argued, gender is simply a performative effect, something which the body does. In this respect, what are we actually eroticising in our sexual partners? When we describe someone as sexually attractive, what is the 'attractiveness'?

One of the cultural practices that has attempted to draw attention to how heterosexuality is premised on the flimsy scaffold of gender is the performance spectacle known as drag. There are, of course, two types of drag. On the one hand, there is the vulgar, 'end-of-the-pier' drag which is obviously a man in female clothing. That type of drag does not subvert or challenge anything as it is clearly a man dressed up. The more challenging form of drag is the seamless, virtuoso performance in which the drag artist performs impeccable femininity.

How we read the politics of an accomplished drag performance is open to debate. Prior to the publication of Butler's *Gender Trouble*, drag was most commonly read as a finely tuned mockery of femininity. Many critics would argue that drag was grounded in misogyny. One argument was that drag performances, which represent caricatured or over-the-top femininity, could be interpreted as a misogynist attack on femininity; an attempt to ridicule feminine acts. Arguably, this was a male body making fun of the excesses of femininity and caricaturing the feminine body. The second argument read an element of male chauvinism in drag since the performance can be interpreted as showing that men can do femininity even *better* than women. This was an argument which was often levelled at many Hollywood cross-dressing performances, for example *Tootsie* (see Bruzzi 1997: 156).

However, Butler challenged these arguments by contending that drag could be celebrated as an activity which draws attention to how all gender is not only performative but also iterative. The virtuoso drag artist demonstrates that femininity is not the essential property of the female body but that it is an act or a doing – a cultural regime. Drag is showing that *all* gender is a performative act, something which bodies do, and therefore it cannot be ridiculing women given that femininity is not their essential act anymore than masculinity is the essential act of men. In this respect, queer theory reads drag as a critique of how bodies are coerced into specific gender acts by culture. Drag de-essentialises or queers gender roles.

As we've already pointed out, queer theory is not simply concerned with gender politics but also how these are related to sexuality. If we consider an image of a virtuoso drag we may find that it is a very 'unsettling' representation. If you are male, and identify as heterosexual, this image could be a rather challenging representation as you may well find this body sexually attractive. However, to emphasise once again, this is a body which is sexed as male – although it is certainly doing femininity very well. The upsetting thing about this body (certainly for heterosexually identified men) is that it forces us to consider what we actually eroticise in our object of desire. If we are attracted to the gender of our potential partners, but gender is simply a performative effect/a doing, then how secure is the identification 'heterosexuality'? If our sexual identifications are supported by the gender binary, but this gender binary is simply a performative effect, then what actual basis have we for claiming any sort of secure sexual identification at all?

However, if Butler is famous for making us aware of the fluid nature of the gender binary, and how this can challenge our belief in a fixed sexual identification, the theorist who brought a different angle to these debates was the late Eve Kosofsky Sedgwick. Sedgwick was a literary critic who, in the same year as Butler unleashed *Gender Trouble*, published another highly influential book in the incipient field of queer studies: *Epistemology of the Closet*. One of Sedgwick's most influential ideas was to question the importance of the gender binary in issues of sexual attraction. Although the majority of people do, indeed, eroticise gender, a great many other people find different elements equally or more attractive in their sexual partners. For example, many people who engage in BDSM (Bondage, Domination, SadoMasochism) eroticise the specific sensations they attain from the activities and not the gender of the partner who is performing the acts with them. Many people who engage in BDSM are equally happy to enjoy these acts with people of either gender. For example, if someone becomes aroused by being tied up and whipped, it may well be irrelevant as to which gender is performing the act. What the person is eroticising is the sensations of the activity and not the gender of the partner who is inspiring these sensations. Similarly, it would be equally possible to classify sexual identity in terms of, say, frequency of sexual acts – rather than by the gender of the sexual partner. Some people like a lot of sex; some people only occasionally. Surely, it would be just as logical to classify people in terms of how often they have sex as it is to bracket them into hetero- or homosexual? Indeed, in a time when HIV transmission is still an issue, it might make more sense to classify people in terms of the risk factor of specific sexual acts. Hence, it would be perfectly logical to argue that people who engage in penetrative sex (whether this is with men or women) should be classified together, while others who engage in the lower risk activity of oral sex (whether this is with men or women) should be classified together.

One of Sedgwick's most controversial arguments has been to queer the sexual activity of masturbation. If someone is having sex with himself/herself how can that activity be identified as heterosexual? If – technically – heterosexuality is the eroticisation of the gender binary then how does someone engaging in solo sex fit into this identification. Indeed, Sedgwick was famous for using this argument in order to queer her own identification. She famously argued that what *felt* like sex to her was masturbation rather than traditional sexual coitus with her male partner. Therefore she argued that she should not necessarily be labelled as heterosexual given that her erotic preference was for sex on her own (Sedgwick 1998).

The key point of both these agendas – Butler's thesis of gender as performative and Sedgwick questioning why we classify sexual identity in terms of the gender of the sexual partner – challenges the assumed fixed nature of our sexual identifications. What actually *is* heterosexuality? If we eroticise the gender of our sexual partner then we are simply attracted to a flexible fiction, a doing or performative effect. Similarly, if we classify our sexuality in terms of sexual act, then what actually *is* the sexual act? One of the most fascinating aspects of humanity is the wide continuum of sexual desire and sexual practices. How, for example, do we classify someone who is turned on by having custard pies thrown at him or her? Is that person heterosexual or homosexual?

Representations of 'Queerness' in the Media

Until fairly recently, most mainstream media texts would only represent queer bodies on the screen if these bodies were coded as monsters and/or villains. When a body violates regimes of gender, this body upsets the gender matrix and is a discomfort for the majority of people who spend their lives adhering to the rules of the gender binary. Vito Russo's highly influential study, *The Celluloid Closet*, surveys the history of Hollywood representation of queer minorities and points out how queer characters – characters that violate traditional gender acts, such as men doing femininity or women doing masculinity – are coded as objects of humour and/or horror. These characters were, arguably, interpreted as gay and it is fair to argue that the spectator's response of laughter and/or horror was simply homophobia. However, it is not certain what audiences of early Hollywood films were laughing at when they watched a man who was doing femininity. Was the laughter simple homophobia as this character was read as gay? Or were audiences simply responding to the violation of the precious gender binary, the discomfort which arises when a body is not conforming to gender expectations?

More recently, film and the media have started to examine queer identifications and often make them the subject matter of the text's narrative. One film text which caused a considerable stir, in both audiences and critics, was the Neil Jordan thriller *The Crying Game*. Set in the most intense period of IRA terrorism in London, this thriller considered how an ex-IRA man Fergus encounters, and falls in love with, the beautiful and enigmatic Dill. However, the twist in the middle of the film is that the beautiful Dill, who has been performing an exotic and very erotic femininity, is actually sexed as male.

In one of the most famous sequences in contemporary cinema, Dill takes Fergus home to 'her' (pronouns fail us here – so we'll use 'her') flat and they start making love, beginning with the usual sexual foreplay of kisses and caresses. Yet when Dill removes her clothes to reveal a penis between the legs, Fergus is violently sick and flees from the flat. The sequence is remarkable for the way it queers gender, gender propriety and sexual desire. During the seduction process, when Dill was still coded as feminine (for both Fergus and the spectator), she was the most active in the sexual pursuit – pushing Fergus down on to the bed and instructing him on what to do. Then, after the moment of revelation, when Dill was revealed to be a male body, Dill's performance became stereotypically feminine as she started clinging to Fergus, begging him not to leave and demonstrating all the stereotypical traits associated with femininity. This queering of the sex/gender/sexuality continuum is one of the most dizzying moments in contemporary cinema and one which startled quite a few spectators in cinema multiplexes.

However, after Dill's queerness is revealed, it is important to note that Fergus does not want to have anything to do with her. When bodies disturb the sex/gender/sexuality continuum, many people who adhere to hegemonic gender regimes are very perturbed, if not even frightened, of queerness. This is one of the key points to remember about a queer identification in that the label 'queer' was originally a term of abuse used to ostracise the queer subject from the mainstream. One of the main agendas within queer politics has been the reclamation of the label 'queer' from being a term of abuse to an identification of pride. This reclamation drew attention to the structural issue of language demonstrating that words in themselves had no particular power; it was how they were used and, more importantly, by whom.

In this respect, queer is a particularly volatile identity and many people would argue that it should only be a self-appellation. When the non-queer identify someone else as queer then there is still the suggestion of insult and defamation. One of the reasons why queer remains such a difficult identification is that no amount of reclamation can ever remove the label from all those years of insult and abuse. Unless someone has known what it feels like to hear the word 'queer' used as an insult or taunt then there is no point in reclaiming the word with a sense of pride. The point is that the identity queer will always bristle with the shame of all those years of abuse and hatred.

Recently, however, contemporary media has started considering the (personal) politics of queer identified characters, often representing sensitive investigations into what it means to be identified as queer. The contemporary American drama series *Glee* has certainly been one of the first shows to represent queer characters (characters who do not conform to gender propriety and disturb the sex/gender/sexuality continuum) in a sympathetic light. One of *Glee*'s most popular characters has been the football coach, Ms Shannon Beiste. As the rather Dickensian surname suggests, this character often suffers exclusion from regimes of human 'civilisation' because she is a very gender-dissident character. Beiste is female but yet does masculinity remarkably well. Although the body is sexed as female, Beiste acts out masculinity with more competence than most of the male bodies in the series. Yet Coach Beiste identifies as heterosexual and, as can only be expected, has suffered a great deal of bullying and taunts because of her non-conformity to gender propriety. She is also represented as experiencing great difficulties within the regime of traditional hetero-erotics, given that gender is the foundation of eroticism and that she does not conform to salient or hegemonic ideologies of femininity.

One of the most controversial storylines in *Glee* was the episode in which the highly sexed teenage students discovered a technique to help stop their hormonal surges: whenever they felt a bit frisky they simply thought about Coach Beiste. This citing of Beiste as a metaphorical 'cold shower' was, of course, because she did not conform to gender propriety and therefore fell between the gender binary which underpins heterosexuality. Beiste's queerness is erotically numbing. If we traditionally eroticise gender then a body which falls between the categories of masculinity and femininity will fail to fit into normative hetero-erotics.

Of course, given that this is television drama (and interpersonal tension is the essence of drama) the students' hormonal dampening technique was revealed to Coach Beiste and, in a rather tear jerking moment, she spoke about how it hurts to be identified as a queer, 'unacceptable' body that doesn't fit into the normative regime of gender/sexuality. The exclusion and the sense of shame about being identified in this way was made very clear in this episode and, like all of *Glee*'s storylines, dealt with this in a controversial fashion – neither sugar coating nor exploiting the subject. *Glee* is remarkable for its sensitive and nuanced investigation of this character, detailing many of the hardships that this character has experienced but, all the time, maintaining a tone of wry, ironic humour and not simply trapping the character within the politics of pity.

More recently we have seen other sensitive representations of queer bodies on the screen. No longer represented as abject monsters to be feared or laughed at, many texts in popular culture are making valiant attempts to investigate the politics and difficulties of bodies that identify outside the narrow continuum of sex, gender and sexuality. Having said that, however, a cursory glance at any school playground will still reveal children who are savagely policing gender roles and identifying non-traditional acts of gender with the finger-pointing taunt of queer. Queer visibility may be increasing in the media; but how people interpret or negotiate these images is a very different matter.

PART II

Media Case Studies

4 Gender and Post-Feminist Television Drama

In this chapter we explore a range of television dramas in relation to the questions we have been asking about contemporary media and gender. As Hollows and Moseley (2006) point out, the rise of 'female centred drama' in the USA provoked a series of debates over the meanings of the various figures they engendered which initiated a particular (and contested) view of 'post-feminism'. In this chapter we examine these figures. The chapter focuses on US 'quality' dramas which, due to their high production values, have been described by various critics as cinematic television. However, while the aesthetics of these shows may have captivated some film critics, the interesting gender politics raised by many of the representations has also attracted considerable attention. We start with a discussion of the iconic, and award winning, drama *Sex and the City* (1998–2004) and then turn to two more recent productions, *Desperate Housewives* (2004–present) and *Mad Men* (2009–present). This allows us to see how this form of television drama has served as a key site for the maintenance and disruption of gender ideology and to address the range of questions that 'post-feminist' dramas raise for television and media scholarship. As described in Chapter 1, post-feminism holds a key place in the critical lexicon in many recent assessments of the terrain of popular television drama over the past two decades. Particular attention has focussed on those dramas that attend to the contemporary problematics of gender, in terms of gender relations, aesthetics, norms or affects (Thornham and Purvis 2005; Hollows and Moseley 2006; Tasker and Negra 2007; Negra 2009; Milestone and Meyer 2012). All of the television series discussed here are particularly interesting in relation to their elaboration and exploration of contemporary modes of femininity, one of the key points of discussion within media and cultural studies over the term 'post-feminism'.

The series under consideration have been referred to as 'quality drama', a designation that, like post-feminism, raises some key definitional problems:– Who decides on what is considered 'quality'? Is it an issue of economics – of budgets or marketing? Or, perhaps more difficult to judge, is it an issue of aesthetics, style or content? For the purposes of this chapter the definition of 'quality' does not rely on assessments of the content of the shows but rather on the critical and popular reception and perception of the shows as examples of what has been termed 'water cooler' television (Jermyn 2010), that is television which makes people interrupt their working lives to discuss and debate. The television series featured here are also notable for their high production values and their carefully crafted (and highly recognisable) 'branding', which of course links back to the question of economics. In this chapter, however, we concentrate on the 'take up' of the series as sites for commenting on, provoking and exploring gender debates.

It is worth stating at the outset that these series are noticeable for their limited preoccupation with middle-class white women. In this they can be seen as typical of one of the more vexed questions raised around 'post-feminism'. Namely, that whilst some applaud post-feminism as an engagement with multiplicity and a play with identity (Brooks 1998) others note the narrowness of character types in the popular media, especially in the more prestigious 'quality dramas'. The centrality of this white, middle-class faction is by no means coincidental and it, in turn, echoes a point made by Sarah Projansky who suggests that 'white, middle class and heterosexual concerns are central to all Postfeminist discourse' (Projansky 2001). *Sex and the City* is an interesting starting point here in that it conforms to this model and has provoked a debate amongst academics over its significant, and typically contradictory, post-feminist articulation. It can be read as demanding attention as one of the first of a collection of television dramas to elaborate an enlightened image of post-feminism. While earlier representations such as *Ally McBeal* offered a gloomy vision of post-feminist identity (post-feminism as a rejection of all feminism's accomplishments), *Sex and the City*, it is suggested, managed to unite feminism's goals with the playfulness, irony, embrace of glamour and critical self-reflexivity of post-feminism. In this view, *Sex and the City* performed the post-feminist dynamic of maintaining femininity alongside feminism (a feminist identification need not signal a rejection of feminine iconography) and maintaining the plurality of feminist politics as emphasised by the varied personal politics of the quartet of female protagonists who feature in the show.

The show is also notable for its adoption of elements of 'queer' into its narrative. It has been noted that the show celebrates an adoption of elements of a queer lifestyle, in that the four women had innumerable sexual partners yet maintained a sense of support from their colleagues and community. The show was also one of the first to explore the dynamics of heterosexuality (see Gerhard 2005). Nearly every episode featured some 'perversity' which asked the spectator to reconsider the idea of 'normative' heterosexuality (see Richardson et al. 2013). On the other hand the show was criticised for its focus on white, middle-class identity, and the very points which make it appealing to some, in its delight in surface, glamour and an obsession with 'shopping and fucking', for others render it a highly problematic text complicit with vacuous consumer culture and the commodification of identity which has a wider cultural significance in relation to the dominance of neoliberal modalities of both contemporary representations *and* production contexts.

In this chapter we will go on to consider recent directions in 'quality drama', considering both *Desperate Housewives* which, as has been argued elsewhere (Richardson 2006), draws on a range of cultural references from *The Stepford Wives* to the melodramas of Douglas Sirk and which has produced, in one of its central characters, the aptly named Bree van der Kamp – a decidedly camp post-feminist heroine. This reading of the show draws out the gender and sexual politics of life behind the white picket fence. An interrogation of this has been a perennial preoccupation of American film, for example in the work of David Lynch (particularly *Blue Velvet* and *Twin Peaks*) through to Sam Mendes (*American Beauty, Revolutionary Road*). It is this critical 'edge' that we will be focussing on here, considering it in relation to the preoccupations with the home and domesticity which, as described in Chapter 2, are highlighted by Diane Negra, Charlotte Brunsdon and others as key features of post-feminist representations and feminist engagements in television.

Finally we turn to the highly acclaimed series *Mad Men*. This show arguably has a more complex gendered address than *Sex and the City* or *Desperate Housewives*, swapping playful irony with a darker and more ambivalent current of gender politics. This is a particularly interesting series with which to think through gender relations and transformations which have taken place over time because it is set in a very precisely specified past (the first season opens in 1960; subsequent series include highly specific cultural references). This allows the series to look back, but, as we suggest, explicitly through the eyes of the present, a gaze which expresses some of the contradictions and ambivalences of the shifting terrain of gender and sexuality over time. The reading focuses on three key female characters, Betty Draper (WASP beauty and suburban housewife) and the 'working girls' Joan Holloway and Peggy

Olson. It tracks how they have been 'taken up' through media commentary as (variously) descriptors of contemporary gender relations in the workplace and at home, and as embodiments of feminine aspiration.

Quintessentially Post-Feminist? From *Sex and the City* to *Mad Men*

As we encountered in Chapter 2 contemporary media scholarship concerned with gender representations has been dominated by explorations and discussions of the complex terrain of 'post-feminism'. Bearing the arguments in mind over whether we understand post-feminism to be primarily hostile to feminism or to be an extension of it, is it a 'backlash' discourse which prematurely announces the welcome end of feminism since the 'battle of the sexes' is over and equality has been achieved? Is it a welcome addition to the 'posts' of post-structuralist, postmodernism and post-colonialism, building on and contributing to their insights? Or, by contrast, should we see it as a disquieting attempt to 'dress up' both long-standing and, conversely, generationally specific antipathies to feminism in (appropriately) new clothes? Post-feminism is viewed by some critics as a recapitulation to very traditional versions of domestic ideology and a reaffirmation of femininity as a 'property of the body'. Conversely, others read it as a playful, not to say raucous, reappropriation of the most traditional features of femininity in a knowing, ironic and highly reflexive mode. These contradictory designations of post-feminism are important features of the critical debate over the term, but in this chapter we are interested in exploring in more detail the figures, particularly the female figures, who populate the post-feminist media landscape.

We take as our case study television drama, in part because it has proved fertile ground for precisely the arguments over what constitutes post-feminism itself. In this respect television drama appears implicated in the construction as well as, perhaps, the reflection of a zeitgeist. Additionally, this form of media, with its relative cultural weight, high profile and frequently high production values, elicits both a range of reflections in other areas of the media, but also interesting identifications and disidentifications on the part of audiences. Perhaps this occurs because of the ways in which characters and situations are allowed to develop over time, producing a more protracted set of engagements. Recent empirical investigations into a female journalist's experience of the media industry has found uses of *Sex and the City* as a sort of cultural shorthand for a particular kind of unashamed relishing of fashion and traditional glamorous embodiments of femininity used as evidence of the 'new' regime of female empowerment (Oliver 2010). The debates about *Sex and the City* spawned an interestingly large number of academic papers which, in part highlighting the epistemological questions raised by feminist research methods, also highlighted the ways in which academic interest in the series sat, sometimes uneasily, with pleasurable identifications of the commentator as fan. In particular, Kim Akass and Janet McCabe's (2004) collection of essays on the series highlights their own engagement as audience members rather than as 'merely' critics. Deborah Jermyn, in her essay in the collection, conducted audience research in which she herself was rather ambiguously positioned as both academic researcher and audience member, or even fan. As we examined in Chapter 2, the debate over popular culture, feminism and feminine identifications has a long history in feminist television scholarship. In part this debate has turned on the reappraisal or reclamation of the feminine in a popular culture which is so often defined negatively in those terms. In this view, a critically denigrated mass culture is defined *as* feminine (Huyssen 1988).

The use of television drama as an index of current dilemmas and debates in relation to a range of issues, particularly to gender and sexuality, is also a feature of discussion of *Mad Men*. Milestone and Meyer (2012) highlight the series' preoccupation with women's changing roles, ambitions and experiences of the workplace in the last 50 years. The series also utilises a high degree of reflexivity (another post-feminist and postmodernist trait) in its attention to a particular precision in its re-creation of the Madison Avenue of the 1960s, viewed from a distinctly 21st-century perspective. This perspective, with respect to gender, means that the series' preoccupation with the central male characters (as the series title indicates), many of whom are explicitly exploitative of women, appears to assume a critical perspective whilst simultaneously revelling in the explicitly exaggerated codes of what we might see as hegemonic forms of masculinity and what one theorist has called 'emphasised' femininity (Connell 1987). Taken together, these series exemplify one of post-feminism's most characteristic features: a contradictory articulation of progressive and regressive elements of gendered identities and identifications played out against a lush backdrop of conspicuous consumption, which is similarly ambivalent in its appeal.

Post-Feminist Genres and Television Contexts

This last point echoes that raised by a number of commentators who note that while some genres seem to 'exemplify' post-feminist themes ('chick flicks', 'rom-coms', female centred television dramas and makeover shows in particular) and have garnered a great deal of attention in relation to their articulation of a 'postfeminist sensibility' (Gill 2007) post-feminism's 'effects' should be understood to operate across a wide range of media genres (Tasker and Negra 2007: 107), including those which do not immediately appear to relate to the post-feminist canon. This suggests that post-feminism can be usefully read in relation to media as both a representational strategy and a discursive construction (Projansky 2001). However, as we saw in the chapter one, feminist television criticism has been uniquely marked by its encounters with the figure of the 'housewife', a figure who can be said to 'haunt' these shows. Whilst it is important to note the wider range of contemporary female figures now populating the post-feminist television landscape – 'a group of women who are notably contradictory in their appeal as powerful action heroines, CEOs, working girls, school girl "vamps", and above all, women fully at home in consumer culture' (Brunsdon and Spigel 2008: 2), and who are far from disappearing – the figure of the 'housewife' and the lure of the domestic maintains a strong hold on the representational regimes of these television dramas, such that, even when this seems to be explicitly abandoned (*Sex and the City*), ironised (*Desperate Housewives*) or pathologised (*Mad Men*), they maintain a crucial cultural presence. So, whilst post-feminist figures should certainly not be reduced to those populating US drama series, nonetheless the high media and cultural profile of these shows does mean that they continue to merit some attention.

The conditions of production and consumption of the dramas under consideration here needs to be part of any comprehensive analysis of the shows, and clearly broad processes such as globalisation, deregulation and consolidation of the media industries which produce the shows and distribute them to a global audience are key features. Attention also needs to be paid to the conditions of reception. As Brunsdon and Spigel put it: 'even if Postfeminist TV dramas circulate on a global market, the meanings of Postfeminism depend on the wider social and political context in which the programmes are viewed' (ibid.: 3). In a related argument, drawing on the work of Foucault on 'governmentality', Martin Roberts suggests that the role and purpose of television is changing with the spheres of public and private now merging:

'privatization, deregulation and technological change have left public service monopolies increasingly having to compete with transnational commercial networks for audiences, while those networks in turn lay claim to the public sphere blurring the distinction between public and private ' (Roberts 2007: 227). This, he argues, is the institutional context for the production of 'lifestyle television' (see Chapter 5 on makeover programming) where, as Gareth Palmer writes, 'the concepts of lifestyle and surveillance are part of a new discursive formation in which appearance is of paramount importance' (quoted in ibid.: 228). Roberts identifies a broad shift from state (politics) to capital (economics), though of course these are interrelated in terms of media. He suggests that corporate interests are served through the privatised and commercialised 'public' spaces of television, which then intervene in the most 'personal' of spaces, that of the 'self'. Roberts's argument specifically refers to 'lifestyle genres'. However, it is also relevant to reading television dramas in which consumption plays such a key role in the performance and maintenance of gender. In this context, gender is a key consideration because of the ways that it interpellates men and women differently as consumers (a point made explicitly in the narrative of *Mad Men* which tracks the emergence of precisely this interpellation in advertising).

Roberts suggests that if feminism, historically, is aligned with a Marxist critique of consumer society and an analysis of the ways in which capitalism 'commodifies' women's bodies and their reproductive labour in terms of the production of 'femininity' through forms of consumption (fashion, cosmetics, etc.), then post-feminist discourses reverse this, reinscribing a model of feminine identity and 'empowerment' organised around consumption. In this way 'a governmentality of gender – the conduct of female conduct' (ibid.: 229) is crucial to maintaining the mass consumption on which postmodern capitalism depends. Gender identities then are understood as produced in accordance with corporate interest which may also unsettle some of those certainties in relation to masculine and feminine elements, for example the feminised but straight, commodity fetishist 'metrosexual'. Relatedly, across a range of media contexts, 'discourses having to do with women's geographic, professional, and perhaps most particularly sexual freedom are effectively harnessed to individualism and consumerism' (Tasker and Negra 2005: 107).

This period has also seen major transformations in the television industries and its associated institutions, as well as in relation to the ways in which it is watched. These dramas reflect some of those changes. For example, we have included the series *Mad Men* for discussion here despite its very low audience figures in the UK (recall that this book is located in this audience perspective). It has been included in part *because* the series has elicited such a lot of media coverage, particularly in the broadsheet newspapers and the middlebrow tabloids, whilst occupying a highly niche position in the marketplace (or to put it another way, very low viewing figures but on a 'highbrow' channel, the BBC's arts oriented BBC4). In this context the various commercial tie-ins of the series are relevant; for example, the high profile fashion launch of *Mad Men* inspired clothing at the high street fashion retailer Banana Republic. These tie-ins demonstrate some of the new conditions of television-inspired marketing, linking the series to its makeover sister genres. The existence of the Banana Republic collection is interesting as testimony to *either* the indifference of global brands to local consumer tastes (the collection was launched in the UK despite the relative failure of the series to garner a substantial audience) *or* the perception that this particular niche market is the one that matters because it is the one with consumer (spending) power. The move from the public service provider (BBC) to the subscription-only Sky for the fifth series also garnered considerable media comment and indicates some of the new reception contexts for television drama. Many media commentators also suggest that the way that television series are viewed has changed, that 'box set' DVDs are the preferred mode, narrowing the gap between feature films and broadcast output.

The fragmentation of television from the (in the UK) public service model (through which commercial television as well as the BBC is regulated) to a multichannel environment with a variety of delivery systems has resulted, increasingly, in 'narrow casting', the development of niche over national publics. Audiences, it is understood in this view, gather around 'social formations of taste' rather than as families, and increasingly there is evidence of the cultivation and development of niche consumer publics clustered around the concept of cosmopolitan lifestyles, fashion, etc., as we can see with the *Mad Men*/Banana Republic tie-in.

Regarding analysis relating to gender this is an interesting development, in that the understanding of television's role in the reproduction and maintenance of a highly normative model of the nuclear (and by extension the national) family has interested scholars (Ticknell 2005). This interest, in part, relates to the traditional address of television, imagining its audience and their viewing habits in familial terms, though these questions are also pertinent to the content of particular kinds of programming. Some television drama interrogates these norms and modes of address. Dramas such as *The L Word* and *Queer as Folk* offer new figures in familial settings which explicitly do not revolve around heterosexual units, and critical discussion of these shows has followed suit. Within this critical context, we turn now to the texts themselves and how they have been read, interrogating the 'post-feminist' figures in television drama with specific reference to how these relate to debates over the ideological territory of the domestic and the neoliberal equation of the production of the self through the language and practices of conspicuous consumption.

Sex and the City

Set in Manhattan, *Sex and the City* was a Home Box Office (cable and satellite network) series which followed the lives of four economically independent and highly privileged female friends. The series was notable for its explicit sexual content and its high adrenaline shopping (see Richardson et al. 2013). Writing during the height of *Sex and the City*'s popularity Diane Negra's reading of the series argued that it needs to be put in its cultural and institutional context. She suggests that it is 'a television series that operates as a key cultural paradigm through which discussions of femininity, single hood, and urban life are carried out' (Negra 2004: 1). She argues that it needs to be considered in relation to many other shows which assumed that single status for women equates automatically to a social problem. For example, the *Bridget Jones's Diary* films and *Ally McBeal* focussed on contradictory feminine figures who both assumed and expected a life lived in the public sphere, and yet who also seem to crave, in fantasy, the traditional resolution of fulfilment through heterosexual romance. They are subject to a rampaging 'biological clock' which means their lives are anxiously (albeit also comically) lived in the shadow of an impending apparent negation, independence quickly turning to something akin to alienation. Negra identifies the cultural context against which these texts should be read as characterised by 'the most intense cultural coercion for women to retreat from the workplace since the post WW2 period' (ibid.: 3). For example, noting the rise of highly elaborate and costly weddings she argues that, more generally, 'retreatism', the withdrawal of women from the public sphere of work into the private sphere of the home, is a widespread 'narrative trope' (Negra 2009). Against *this* background *Sex and the City* 'bespeaks a desire to probe this cultural script, even if ultimately the series seldom musters a fully fledged critique' (Negra 2004: 7). Citing an instalment where Charlotte gets married ('Don't Ask Don't Tell'), Negra argues that the episode 'asks probing questions about the pretence, performativity and self-deception that can underwrite bridal ritualization', which critically interrogates Charlotte's desire 'to be the idealized/commodified bride our culture celebrates'. Negra suggests that unlike other 'chick flicks or 'chick lit' the series avoids the 'renunciation narrative' and offers less finality, keeping open the possibilities for hope and regret and ambivalence.

Another key aspect of the series is its setting in New York which perhaps 'licenses' the display of a form of unruly femininity through its specialised locale, its cosmopolitan location (see Richardson et al. 2013). Negra suggests that this setting and indeed the obsessions the series revels in, shopping and fashion, means that the character's subjectivity is defined through and by these experiences and this location: 'the emphasis on such a setting may run the risk of deflecting attention from the alienation and diminished citizenship of single women who exist in a variety of class categories and geographical locations and whose lives play out at a significant remove from the luxury and consumerist pleasures … highlighted by the series' (Negra 2004: 23).

Thornham and Purvis (2005) make a similar point when they argue that whilst the series seems to offer an empowering, and even transgressive, narrative there are many contradictory elements in the show, which means that it conforms to as many norms as it breaches. It is true that *Sex and the City* frequently reverses the gaze, so that men as well as women are objectified by the camera and are made to look both ridiculous and disempowered, and the series does revel in the centrality of the women who are living single, fulfilling and independent lives, which are unique to the era after second-wave feminism (in this, at least, it is certainly a post-feminist text), and who rely more on each other than on men. Yet, on the other hand, the series is unashamedly romantic, and the fantasies which underpin it are often explicitly 'fairytales' – though with the playful ironising that is a feature of post-feminism (which, as both Rosalind Gill (2007) and Imelda Whelehan (2000) have argued, often performs a very useful alibi for sexism). They conclude that 'this is a world … in which the personal is the only form of politics and the encounters … with social and class difference … [are] encounters with dream fantasy and image' (Thornham and Purvis 2005: 128).

Others note that the pleasures of watching *Sex and the City* are often communal, shared with female friends (Jermyn 2004) and that there are familiar dangers in dismissing the pleasures of consumption and feminine identified pleasure. They further note that the emphasis on sexuality as myriad, as performance and as play is, in itself, quietly revolutionary; especially when those playing are women. However, in this regard the series can also be seen to have very particular limits. Despite the oft-repeated mantra of Samantha's that 'women can now have sex like men' it is notable that the series is somewhat uncomfortable with lesbianism. Mandy Merck makes precisely this point, noting the series' 'abjection of female homoeroticism' (2004), despite its never ending tease. Merck's reading points to the origins of the series in Candace Bushnell's column in the *New York Observer* and notes that these columns were overwhelmingly male rather than female centred and that the solidarity of the female friends, which plays such a key role in the series and its critical reception, is conspicuous by its absence: 'Bushnell's columns are mostly about men, successful Manhattan men and their deep antagonism to women ... contact with other women is sporadic, rivalrous and often downright hostile' (ibid.: 49). Describing Bushnell's version of New York as a 'heterosexual hell in which men and women continually pursue and repel each other until they settle in to hellish marriages', it is notable that the series has been taken up so thoroughly in terms of its celebration of female bonds.

These bonds are also interesting for their rejection of lesbianism, as Merck points out, noting that the only fully fledged lesbian affair for one of the quartet goes to the 'libertine' Samantha and 'the combination of her emotional attention deficit disorder and the series' overall heterosexism dooms the affair' (ibid.: 57). Despite its coyness over lesbianism, however, Merck also points to the ways that the show does display a 'gay sensibility', in part through its authorship, with gay men credited by Bushell with its creation, its artsy/metropolitan milieu and also through a highly camp emphasis on the rituals associated with the production of gender, which emphasises the links between various appropriations of drag, linguistic as well as sartorial. Linking the camp preoccupations of the series to the points raised earlier about post-feminism, the relation between consumption and identity is particularly striking and references the perception (far from the reality for many gay men) of 'fabled prosperity and discernment supposedly offer[ing] the consuming power of both sexes – money *and* taste' (ibid:60). Commentators on the series made the point that the quartet of women had much akin with gay men but were more 'ratings friendly', leading Merck to conclude that '*Sex and the City* makes its women not the fantasy partners but the fantasy equivalents of metropolitan gay men' and in regard to the sexuality of the series that 'if the content is straight the form is gay' (ibid: 62).

In relation to gender and sexuality, then, the series can be read as very much a site of 'intense cultural negotiation' (Pender, cited in Purvis and Thornham: 129), offering female figures who seemed to offer something novel in the production, reproduction and articulation of gender and sexuality on television. Certainly the series generated enormous discussion about its novelty. If the series did seem to exemplify a very particular moment of a 'post-feminist sensibility' – in its emphasis on (hetero) sexual liberation, its only semi-ironic obsession with unbelievably expensive shoes as the true fruit of second-wave feminism – then it looks from 2014 to be a moment of historically conspicuous (fantasy) consumption which even at the time was notable for its exclusions and class hierarchies but whose moment also seems well and truly over in the post-2008 new economic order.

Desperate Housewives

Sex and the City's interest lies in its post-feminist contradictions, both probing and conforming to the cultural scripts of femininity, and transgressing and reinforcing tropes of femininity and consumption. The show obviously views marriage and romance as the ultimate goal even as they are explicitly deconstructed (as in the representation of lawyer Miranda's far from idyllic maternity). It offers an apparently queer sensibility but shies away from female homoeroticism. Contrasting the series with *Desperate Housewives*, the latter seems initially to suggest even less fertile ground for a progressive gender articulation. The title itself speaks to a seemingly retrograde assumption. The iconic centrality of the term 'housewife' seems positively anachronistic, given the ongoing difficulties faced by women in achieving parity in the workplace and the enduring economic necessity for the vast majority of women to work outside of the home. But here, in a much less risqué series, similar elements of both transgression and affirmation of suburban gender values can be discerned.

This series seems to beg the question as to whether the bourgeoise milieu, the picture-perfect white-picket-fenced land of Wisteria Lane, is being sent up, ironised or validated and reified? Similarly, is there is a critique here around the ideology of domesticity? In the first series this certainly seemed plausible given the suicide which inaugurated the series and drove much of the narrative. In some ways the series seemed to resemble the deconstruction of US suburbia that had been a hallmark of much of David Lynch's output (*Blue Velvet* for example and the surreal murder mystery *Twin Peaks*). The series also seems to owe (see Richardson, 2006) a debt to the master of melodrama Douglas Sirk, whose films have been read as searing critiques of bourgeois values and US capitalism (Mulvey; 1987 Elsaesser 1987). US culture, particularly in its 'women's genres' (the melodrama and the 'women's film'), have been understood by many critics as marked by a complex dissection of the fantasy and reality of the suburban ideal and its perverse and patholog- ical underside. The heterosexual family unit is firmly under scrutiny as the emblem and generator of misery and alienation under and behind the veneer of bourgeois respectability and lush material settings. Sam Mendes's films, *American Beauty* and *Revolutionary Road*, and Todd Haynes's homage to Sirk, *Far From Heaven* and his television adaptation of the noir/melodrama hybrid *Mildred Pierce*, are more recent examples of this. Whilst *Desperate Housewives* neither aspires to nor produces this kind of searing critique of the family it is still worth considering for its portrayal of gender and sexuality which highlight a post-feminist aesthetic which both seems to embrace traditional modes of femininity whilst undermining any claim to feminine essence. As with *Sex and the City* the delight in surface over depth reveals gender as a style, rather than as an abiding substance (Butler 1990), and the knowing, ironic distance is typical of a particularly camp appeal (Richardson 2006).

It could be suggested (ibid.) that we take into account the production team and their gender and sexual politics in an analysis of the series as exhibiting a sensibility which is best understood as definitely (and defi- antly) camp. We might point out that 'camp' has traditionally been allied to, and indeed treasured by, homosexual men as a reworking of the cultural symbolic, in part to reify surface over so-called 'depth'. Disrupting the normative (and normalising) supposed continuities between sex, sexuality and gender, camp is achieved through the dynamics of appropriation, pastiche and irony. In *Desperate Housewives* we see something interesting emerging, which links to post-feminism in the use of a camp aesthetic in relation especially to one of the female characters, the appropriately named Bree van der Kamp (ibid.). In such a reading, Bree's femininity (importantly for the discussion here in rela- tion to her role as homemaker extraordinaire) is revealed as just as arti- ficial as any male appropriation of the feminine, that is as drag. This shows up the arguments made by Judith Butler that all gender should be understood as performative, that is to say produced and performed, in both conscious and unconscious ways, through ritual and citation, which in its doing comes to be – rather than expressing some pre-exist- ing self, sex or truth.

In its deconstruction of the myths of essential femininity and its relation to the home, then, the series premise bring us back to one of the issues faced by feminist critics of post-feminist television. Namely, how to read and respond to the reworking of domestic ideology and the apparently regressive and traditional elements of the cult of motherhood through an embracing of those styles and performances but with the element of irony and distance firmly in place. The fashion for retro, 1950s teashops, burlesque and cupcakes have arguably combined in interesting ways to made baking and housewifery glamorous. On the one hand, this can be related to the points that Diane Negra makes with regard to the 'retreatism' she perceives as a strong cultural emphasis which typifies much of the post-feminist discursive rejection of what are taken to be the goals of second-wave feminism: 'having it all' (Negra 2004, 2009). Charlotte Brunsdon argues that the recuperation of domesticity evidenced for example in Nigella Lawson's *How to be a Domestic Goddess* is premised on a 'dis-identification' with the 'deranged superwoman' beloved of post-feminist discourse as a caricature of 'second wave feminism's' aims (Brunsdon 2006). In this context, what is striking is the way that *Desperate Housewives* undermines this premise. As its title indicates, the women of Wisteria Lane are far from living the idyll. To return to Richardson's reading, he points to the ways in which both motherhood and aggressive domestic competence are revealed as only marginally and intermittently rewarding. Undercutting and ironising the symbolism of 1950s' iconography, post-feminist fictions reveal the contradictions of domesticity and highlight the fact that, even in the 1950s, this was never simple. Patricia Mellencamp's reading of the 1950s' sitcom *I Love Lucy* shows how Lucy's clowning in the kitchen allowed the comedy to provide a way of both articulating the desire to escape the confines of domesticity while ritually reinstalling its centrality (Mellencamp, 1992). Perhaps *Desperate Housewives* can be read as similarly ambivalent in its domestic orientation.

Mad Men

If *Desperate Housewives* offers an ambivalent picture of domesticity and its discontents (to paraphrase Freud) and *Sex and the City* offers a version of femininity which gains its meaning in part by contrast with its domestic 'others', then the glossy and self-consciously sophisticated *Mad Men* similarly plays out the politics of gender through female figures with contrasting emotional investments in hearth, home and workplace. Interestingly the series has been taken up in the UK media in ways which relate quite explicitly to the debates and dilemmas so far discussed over post-feminism's contradictory articulations. This reading will use some of the coverage from the UK's liberal broadsheet newspaper *The Guardian* and the notoriously right-wing *Daily Mail* to highlight some of these contradictions, noting how the take up of the series in media commentary picks up on the currency of this 'period piece', specifically in relation to contemporary gender and sexual politics. Like *Sex and the City* and *Desperate Housewives* the series is only really interested in its white, privileged characters. However, for some commentators, the interest in the series has been the way it ambivalently offers the viewer either a deconstruction of this norm or, conversely, a nostalgic celebration of it, resulting in the symbolic sedimentation of privilege.

The series has garnered enormous praise for its stylish and caustic appraisal of the advertising industry and its 'mad men'. The title refers to the location, Madison Avenue in New York, yet also clearly signals a specifically masculine world on which the viewer is invited to cast a somewhat jaundiced eye. This section will concentrate on two of the key elements in relation to gender that have been highlighted in the British press: firstly, the debate over whether the show, in its loving recreation of a pre-second-wave feminist world, is itself misogynist or sexist; secondly, the discussions generated by the series in relation to costume, fashion and the female body. These debates are, of course, already familiar in relation to the themes of post-feminist discourse already discussed. However, *Mad Men*'s period setting gives a distinct dimension to the representation of (amongst other things) gender relations, working conditions, sexual violence and gender embodiment.

Three key female figures in the series exemplify some of these themes (that they can be so neatly categorised is itself telling). Betty, in the first few series, is the wife of the central character, Don Draper. She is a beautiful, suburban housewife and mother, routinely equated with Hitchcock's blonde heroines, Grace Kelly and Tippi Hedren. Peggy Olson, by contrast, faces a difficult career and personal trajectory in the man's world of advertising. She manages, despite an unplanned pregnancy, to make a break from secretarial work and move into copywriting. Joan Holloway is a senior secretary in the firm whose affair with her boss and subsequent marriage to a man who rapes her in the office has been an element of the press's interest. Tellingly, however, rather more column inches have been devoted to her 'hourglass figure' and its fashioning. If fashion is indeed the fifth character in *Sex and the City* (Bruzzi and Church Gibson 2004), then it should certainly also be added to the cast list of *Mad Men*.

If lifestyle television is producing (or inventing) contemporary masculinities not incompatible with grooming, cooking and fashion then period fictions such as *Mad Men* are interesting in their recourse to other, more traditional, templates of masculinity and femininity. Here, the sartorial styling of the men (every bit as elegant and glamorous as the women, in fact) is harnessed to status and work. The series's narrative and thematic interest in the shifting gender relations of the time in which it is set (the early 1960s) enables it to utilise the audience's hindsight to read these sartorial signals in interesting ways. Much of the press coverage of the show has revolved around wardrobe issues, including much discussion of the corsetry and underwear fetishisation of the pencil skirted office manager, Joan Holloway (played by Christina Hendrick). The series's delight in this 'double vision' also extends to its knowingness in regard to certain aspects of second-wave feminism. Set in a Madison Avenue advertising office the series is immersed in the world of consumption and marketing in ways which link it to post-feminist discourse. This happens both within the diegesis through an exposé of the manufacture of desire at the heart of capitalist consumer culture and in relation to *Mad Men* itself as a commodity used to sell other commodities via the marketing of retro fashion in the high street. However, the press coverage of the female fashions of the early 1960s displayed in the series go rather further than a simple delight in retro chic. The costumes themselves are linked through media discourse to discussions about women's contemporary status as sexual objects, body anxiety and cosmetic surgery.

The *Daily Mail* on 30 January 2011 ran the headline 'Curvy Mad Men Star Christina Hendricks Fuels Demand for Breast Enlargements'. The article itself quotes the comments of Lynn Featherstone, at the time the government's equalities minister who explicitly singled out Hendrick's body type as a more appropriate ideal than the ultra-slim 'size 0' models so beloved of the popular press's schizophrenic fascination with idealising and berating women's bodies. The *Daily Mail* quotes figures from the British Association of Aesthetic Plastic Surgeons who reported a 10 per cent increase in breast enlargement operations (nearly 10,000 operations), allegedly as a result of 'the Christina Hendricks effect'. The discursive move here seems to be to normalise the process by which identification and admiration for particular body types translates into surgical procedures. This is a point which has been made by Virginia Blum (2003) in her argument that celebrity and surgical culture are inextricably linked.

The *Daily Mail*'s general excitement over the series, its costumes and what they might symbolise (which turns out to be a somewhat incoherent and contradictory highly sexualised kind of empowered subordination) is evident in a feature which involves a *Mad Men* 'makeover' entitled 'How to Drive Men Mad' (Power 2012). This article identifies the work involved in producing the look of the show and the effect it has (predictably) on men: 'there's no leering, no jeering – these men are putty in my hand'. However, the author also points out just how exhausting the whole process is, and how very uncomfortable it is: 'as the day goes on, I get tired. My bra is suffocating me, the waistband of my girdle is digging into my tummy and the tops of my thighs are rubbing uncomfortably together'. However, the article ends with the point that returning to 'normal' clothes entails a loss of this empowered femininity which produces something of a gender crisis – 'I am like a completely different woman. Actually I don't really feel like a woman at all' – and suggests that the invisibility which comes with not donning the mad outfits makes her 'sad'.

The show's apparent ability to get women to rethink their attachments to traditionally female symbols and roles is also evident in the *Daily Mail*'s coverage of social trends apparently related to the series in reports such as 'Mad Men Boosts Trend of Secretary Title' (*Daily Mail*, 5 April 2012). This was apparently based on a finding by the International Association of Administration Professionals which 'said it detected a two fold increase in the uptake of the title "secretary" reversing a twenty year decline in the use of the title speculating that the series has provoked nostalgia for the image'. Reporting these particular 'trends' fits quite neatly with the *Mail*'s interest in traditional gender roles and ideologies as well as exemplifying a post-feminist appreciation for self-identification with traditional formulations and expressions of femininity. However, the utilisation of the series for an array of 'gender stories' in the press is, in itself, suggestive.

Debate spawned in the show over gender roles and expression find a rather different form on the pages of the 'progressive' *Guardian* newspaper. Here, Featherstone's remarks about Hendricks are taken up by pointing out the inconsistency of an equalities minister 'obsessing about feminine beauty' and admonishing her to 'concentrate on helping young girls think about the size of their achievements rather than the flatness of their navels' (Hill 2010). However, the paper has returned over and over again to the question of whether, in producing a show which so starkly represents the inequalities of the past, it doesn't, in fact, indulge in a particular version of misogyny itself.

This is an interesting question for gender and media since it gets to the heart of why representations matter and also how complex representations of gender actually are. The paper's continual revisiting of this question seems to be symptomatic of the question itself being perhaps the point, in that, like *Sex and the City*, the series might be read as a site of cultural negotiation over precisely these kinds of questions. *Mad Men*'s re-creation of a workplace in which women and (closeted) gay men are routinely demeaned and exploited, and a suburbia which quite literally makes housewives sick, can and has been read as either contesting or reproducing these tropes (in a familiar, post-feminist, have it both ways, fashion).

To illustrate this we could look at one memorable scene (series 2, episode 7) where, on returning from a particularly horrendous evening, Betty Draper vomits over her husband's new Cadillac, the none too subtle gendered symbol of (for Don Draper) class mobility, sexuality and mid-life crisis. The vomiting occurs at a point where Betty is forced to acknowledge her husband's infidelities, which she has hitherto been able successfully to disavow, and can be read as a powerful statement of the sickening effect of this particularly unhappy marriage. That the marriage and family might also be read as a symbol of a wider cultural malaise is also indicated in the same episode where the Draper family take the new car on a picnic outing. The apparently idyllic family moment is undercut by a long static shot of the picnic field after the Drapers have left. Their picnic rubbish strewn over the ground offers a view of not only the emergence of a 'throwaway' and disposable culture with its concomitant environmental degradation but, taken together with Betty's despoiling of the car's interior, also appears to link this rampant consumption explicitly to the pathologies of the traditional heteronormative nuclear family.

Much of *The Guardian*'s coverage of Betty notes the coincidence of her name to the writer of the classic feminist deconstruction of 'the feminine mystique' – and it is Betty Friedan's characterisation of the American suburban housewife, as locked into a 'comfortable concentration camp', that seems to haunt *Guardian* feature writers discussing the series.

Sandy Doyle, in an article entitled 'Mad Men's Feminine Mystique' (2009), notes the double edged re-creation of a belief system based on white male privilege: 'of course it's also a belief system for which there's a great deal of nostalgia. *Mad Men* has its glamour ... but its great accomplishment is in how it gives the lie to the conservative long-ing for "traditional" values by portraying the time as almost unthink-ably dark for all involved, including the men in charge' (Doyle 2009).

Kira Cochrane, also in response to the first two series, makes a simi-lar argument, charting her own initial revulsion at the way the series seemed to 'heroise [*sic*] the nasty sexists of Stirling Cooper, the ad agency at the centre of the show, while suggesting that the women were entirely complicit in their oppression'. However, she suggests that on a second (box-setted) viewing it was instead 'critiquing the chauvinism and often outright misogyny of the year 1960'. (2009)

Katherine Whitehorn's discussion makes another explicit connection to Friedan, suggesting that the series demonstrates 'why it shouldn't have surprised anybody' that '*The Feminine Mystique* lit such a forest fire'(2009). And the novelist Lionel Shriver in an article entitled 'Beautiful Betty: A Warning from Home Making History' (2010) again makes the explicit link to the ideology of the housewife and the contemporary discussion of the choices women face in reclaiming their domestic role and, following the familiar pattern with all of these commentaries, links the series to contemporary gender politics. She suggests that 'any woman seriously considering the new "freedom" to choose housewifery and motherhood as a substitute for a demanding career should watch every episode of *Mad Men* back to back, perusing the re-issue of the Feminine Mystique during the adverts' (ibid).

Male commentators, too, have discussed the series in relation to its construction and deconstruction of the politics of gender. *The Guardian*'s TV blogger Gareth Mclean sums this up in reaction to the first series with the question 'Is Mad Men Misogynistic?':

> Isn't the overall message of the show ... that the alpha male is destined for self destruction? Indeed you might argue that their disintegration means that the men are as much victims of the time in which they live as the women they harass and hate? Isn't the point of mad men that these men, too, are trapped in suffocating gender roles? ... Or is *Mad Men*'s success down to something more sinister? Does it tap into nostalgia for a time when it was acceptable to be sexist, racist and the rest? (2009)

The coverage of the series in the liberal *Guardian* is pertinent to a discus-sion of gender and drama because it addresses the debates that feminist television studies has confronted, over the prevalence and meaning of the housewife in popular cultural forms, and links this to contemporary gender politics. In doing so it also participates in the ongoing negotiations around these issues, demonstrating the ways that drama series provoke contradictory identifications and negotiations in terms of gender and sexuality, even and perhaps especially at the point when these seem most overtly liberatory or conversely regressive.

Conclusion

In this chapter we have examined a range of 'quality' US drama series to explore some of the ways that television series have been read as implicated in the negotiation, contestation and reproduction of the politics of gender and sexuality. All three of these series share an exclusive focus on (almost without exception) white, heterosexual, privileged subjects, and all to some extent can be seen as offering a fantasy transcendence of the everyday. They also share a perspective which is demonstrably post-feminist in that the goals and advances of second-wave feminism are, at least to some extent, assumed, whilst the enduring debates and dilemmas over the playing out of performances of femininity in relation to sexuality, home and work are seemingly perpetually replayed, in both the series themselves and in the wider discussions thus engendered. The series are also interesting for their various articulation of the relationships amongst gender, sexuality and consumption. From *Sex and the City*'s celebration of consumption to *Mad Men*'s deconstruction of the manufacture of desire on which that consumption is partly based might seem a long ideological distance, but the evidence from the high street of *Mad Men*'s easy co-option into consumption practices and the apparent resurgence of identifications with highly traditional modes of femininity should perhaps give us pause to reconsider the complexity of representation and its relation to the construction and reconstruction of the everyday.

5 The Make-Over Show

Once a segment tagged on to a morning television magazine programme, the make-over show has now attained prime-time viewing. Most evenings of the week, there are programmes which are dedicated to telling people how they *should* dress; how they *should* style their bodies; how they *should* diet and exercise; and, most often, how their bodies *should* appear younger than they really are. In short, there is now no shortage of media representation instructing us about how we should look.

One of the things that has changed in the past few decades has been our perception of the body itself. We no longer consider the body to be fixed or innate but as something which is shaped by culture. We are all of us 'body-builders' in that we are all building our bodies on a daily basis. We diet and exercise in order to shape the tissues of our bodies; we apply make-up; we tan or paint our skin in order to achieve a specific skin tone/hue; we shape our silhouettes through our choice of clothes; and we decide how much hair we want on our bodies and shave, wax or pluck. Of course, some of us engage in more extreme practices: we tattoo our bodies; pierce our bodies; build the muscles of our bodies; have laser surgery so that our eyes are no longer myopic; inject botulism poison into our frown lines or have a vacuum pump inserted into our soft tissues to suck out unwanted fat cells. In other words, there is no shortage of procedures which are widely available for people to modify or shape their bodies, and indeed the cultural agenda has now shifted from asking why someone would engage in a body modificatory practice to condemning those who do *not* engage in some 'body-building' activity. Not to engage in the 'necessary' body modification practices is, in many circumstances, culturally frowned upon. The example of the *Britain's Got Talent* finalist – the singer Susan Boyle – is an excellent example of a body that was ridiculed initially because it was ungroomed and unstyled. When Boyle first appeared at the open auditions, the audience dismissed her as yet another talentless fool, largely because this woman had not engaged in styling or building her body in accordance with acceptable cultural regimes. At her audition, Boyle wore clashing clothes (white shoes with black tights), had bushy eyebrows (and, of course, contemporary culture dictates that these *should* be waxed into 'shape'), facial hair (which, again, contemporary culture dictates *should* be removed on a female body) and unstyled, unruly hair. In short, this 'unacceptable' body suggested that the woman's singing performance would match her poor performance of groomed femininity (her performance of being a woman, in fact). So it was staged as one of the greatest television shocks in history when it turned out that Boyle had a beautiful, well-trained singing voice. That a disciplined, immaculately groomed voice could come from such an undisciplined, ungroomed body was presented as such a media shock that Susan Boyle's audition became one of the most watched clips ever on YouTube. Perhaps the treatment of Boyle by the media and the 'public' suggests that it is now unusual to credit an undisciplined body with any talent or ability whatsoever. An ungroomed body – in other words, a body which does not adhere to the cultural requirements of any (sub) culture at all – is culturally dismissed as, at best, eccentric or, at worst, unhinged.

Of course, if the body is the product of cultural regimes, it is important to remember that different body projects are acceptable at different periods and in different contexts. For example, in times of hardship and famine (when food has been scarce) to be fatter, more plump, signified upper-class luxury and was therefore desirable. In contemporary Western culture – a time of fast food aplenty, when we really have too much food rather than too little – the fashionable agenda is now to be thinner. Another example in the change in British body culture is tanning the skin. Over a hundred years ago, it was fashionable to have very pale skin. The signifier of upper (middle) class femininity was alabaster skin – unsoiled by the sun's rays. It was only labourers or peasants, toiling outside for long hours, who would have sun-stained (i.e. tanned) skins. However, by the 1950s, when holidays abroad became the signifier of upper-class affluence, having a summer holiday tan became very fashionable. The tan was the sign that someone could afford a holiday in the Mediterranean rather than make do with a trip to the cloudy British seaside. But, given recent medical evidence of the dangers of sun tanning for Caucasian skin – at the very least it causes the skin to age prematurely and, at worst, can cause skin cancer – there has been a backlash against the summer tan. Indeed, one of the essential items on contemporary culture's shopping list is the skin protection lotion and the sunblock. Yet, the 'look' of tanned skin refuses to leave contemporary white British fashion and so various forms of fake tan are now widely available. Indeed, many people will even discuss what type of tan they wear in the way that, years ago, people would have talked about a shirt or a pair of jeans. In other words, the body is very much held in thrall to contemporary culture and the imperative of fashion regimes builds or shapes the body in the style that is deemed 'acceptable'. These cultural codes of the body continue to be both classed and racialised, making the signification of skin tone, hair and so on subject to specific and contextual regimes, with distinct meanings attached for different groups, invested in specific forms of body maintenance. However, when a body refuses to adhere to these 'local' regimes it is often ridiculed or dismissed as eccentric or a freak (see Richardson 2010 on contemporary media 'enfreakment') – as happened with Susan Boyle on her television debut. Put simply, culture controls and shapes the body.

Of course, when there are cultural regimes at work, there are always strategies of resistance to this cultural hegemony, and such resistance or disobedience is manifested through the body. A teenager's first act of rebellion may well be through hair and he or she will style it in a fashion which is deemed unacceptable by school and parents and perhaps dye it a lurid colour or have it cut into an extreme style. Other acts of resistance which might follow would be getting a tattoo or engaging in some form of body piercing. However, although the rebellious youth may well feel that he or she is making a stand against cultural oppression, it is important to remember that the act of disobedience has simply moved the body into another (sub) cultural regime which has just as many rules and regulations as the mainstream culture. For example, if a body engages in body piercing, that body moves into the subcultural group of 'body piercing enthusiasts' where there are just as many rules and regulations as can be found in mainstream culture. Any subcultural group will have its own codes and conventions about what is deemed acceptable and not acceptable. For example, particular piercings are acceptable in various body parts but not in others. In other words, there is no escaping the grip that culture has upon the body.

Yet, the key question is how is this control, this discipline, of the body maintained in contemporary culture? The theorist who was the first to consider this was the philosopher Michel Foucault who explored the mechanisms by which the body is disciplined and ordered by culture. I now want to outline Foucault's arguments from his very influential text *Discipline and Punish* before then considering how these very mechanisms are mobilised within the spectacle of the makeover TV show.

Foucault argued that, in *premodern* culture, discipline was achieved through the mechanism of physical torture. If bodies were badly behaved or disobedient, the state would sanction official torture in order to discipline these bodies. For example, if the body had committed a minor offence then this body might be placed in the stocks for a day or two. This was a device into which the person's hands and feet were clamped, thus cramping the body in an uncomfortable position, and this torture usually occurred in a public place (the village square) where the guilty person was exhibited as a warning of what could happen to other bodies that performed similar acts. Presumably, the stocks would be a punishment for a relatively minor offence such as theft or an act of public unruliness. On the other hand, the torture could be more extreme and the body could be flagellated, beaten or even forced to endure unbearable sensations such as the thumb-screw or being stretched on the wrack.

The problem with the spectacle of public torture, however, was that it failed to attain its purpose. As a medium of public control, torture was unsuccessful. There were a number of reasons why it didn't work but the most obvious were that it often heroicised the guilty body who was being punished. Watching someone being tortured might have inspired sympathy in the onlookers and the villain was elevated to the status of martyr. Even a cold-blooded murderer could assume heroic status when he was made the spectacle of public torture. Significantly for Foucault's account, torture and other brutal 'sovereign' acts of violence against the transgressive body enacted 'in the name of the king' wracked unbearable sensations on the body but did not affect the core person, the mind of the subject.

Torture was eventually abandoned as a means of public discipline and replaced by the mechanism of imprisonment – a standard of public discipline which is still maintained today. The supreme prison system was the panopticon one – an architectural structure designed by Jeremy Bentham. The panopticon consists of a central warden's tower surrounded by an amphitheatre of prison cells, which are under constant surveillance. The prisoners become aware that every action can be seen by the warden. Eventually the prisoners learn that they are under constant surveillance and *interiorise* the gaze of the warden, in effect becoming their own gaolers or wardens. Indeed, in the panopticon, it becomes irrelevant whether or not the warden is even *in* the tower as every prisoner has internalised the surveillance and becomes a self-policing subject. As Foucault explains, 'there is no need for arms, physical violence, material constraints. Just a gaze. An inspecting gaze, a gaze which each individual under its weight will end by *interiorizing* to the point that he is his own overseer, each individual thus exercising this surveillance over, and against himself' (Foucault 1977: 155, my emphasis).

This mechanism of the panopticon prison system, and the interiorising gaze which it produces, offers the perfect metaphor to illuminate how contemporary body image is policed in culture. From an early age, we become aware that we are constantly under surveillance, policed by the gaze of contemporary culture. Like the inmates in the panopticon we internalise this idea of surveillance and become self-disciplining subjects. Anyone who has ever felt stressed about his or her appearance, or has asked him or herself 'Does my bum look big in this?', has demonstrated an acute awareness of this interiorising of the cultural gaze.

However, as various critics have pointed out, the panoptic gaze of contemporary culture is distinctively gendered. As we pointed out in Chapters 2 and 3, women have historically been thought of simply in terms of their bodies (Spelman 1982). While a male body is appraised in terms of what his body can do, the female body has always been judged in terms of how it looks. In this respect, female bodies are subject to this interiorising gaze much more than male bodies. As Joan Copjec explains, 'the panoptic gaze defines *perfectly* the situation of the woman under patriarchy' (1989: 54). Sandra Bartky, in a much quoted passage, points out some details of this:

> The woman who checks her make-up half a dozen times a day to see if her foundation has caked or her mascara run, who worries that the wind or rain may spoil her hairdo, who looks frequently to see if her stockings have bagged at the ankle, or who, feeling fat, monitors everything she eats, has become, just as surely as the inmate of the panopticon, a self-policing subject, a self committed to a relentless, self-surveillance. This self-surveillance is a form of obedience to patriarchy.
>
> (Bartky 1990: 80)

This gendered imbalance is evident if we consider the most popular dramatisation of the panoptic gaze in popular media: the make-over show. Recent years have seen a huge growth in the number of television make-over shows and nearly all of these are designed to remind a 'disobedient' body that it is in the metaphoric panopticon and should become a self-policing subject. However, this body is *nearly* always female.

One exceptionally popular example of the contemporary make-over show is Channel 4's *Ten Years Younger*. (Originally the show was *Ten Years Younger in Ten Days* but was revised when the ten days became just too much work for the cosmetic surgeon and the make-over victim alike.) The premise of *Ten Years Younger* is very simple: it finds a body (this is nearly always a female body) which has disobeyed the rules of self-surveillance and has 'let herself go'. In order to remind this body that she must pay more attention to the rules of conventional feminine iconography, this body is forced to stand out in the high street (wearing no make-up and dressed in a cheap and nasty fleece) and have one hundred cruel and insensitive members of the public pass hurtful (sometimes downright bitchy) comments about her as they are asked to estimate her age. As if this is not humiliating enough for the poor woman, she then has to listen to all these comments played back for her on a video recording and learn what the public think of her. The comments are usually extremely insensitive, ranging from 'she looks like an old bag woman' to 'mummy, mummy! It's a monster!'. This, of course, all serves to remind the woman that she is an inmate of the panopticon and under the constant surveillance of the warden's gaze (the patriarchal gaze). It should also be noted that there is a distinct trace of premodern torture at work here too, as exhibiting the woman in the public shopping centre is comparable to the public display of the prisoner in the stocks in the medieval village square.

Of course, the premise of *Ten Years Younger* is to imply that the woman *should* not need to be reminded in this cruel fashion because she *should* have internalised the gaze and already be a self-policing subject. The narrative voice-over always suggests this by the way it sensationalises the horrific list of terrible things the woman does to her body, such as over-plucking the eyebrows, back-combing her hair, smoking or (the ultimate, toe-curling horror) forgetting to wear sunblock. This, of course, is pronouncing the woman 'guilty', in the eyes of the spectator, for her neglect of the requirement to be a self-policing subject.

Ten Years Younger, however, then 'solves' this problem by subjecting the woman to a gruelling ordeal of cosmetic surgery and regrooming before a more 'appropriate' body (in other words one which now conforms to 'acceptable' feminine iconography) is revealed at the end. Of course, this programme is only one example of this genre. Cressida Heyes (2007) points out that a similar disciplinary agenda is demonstrated in *Extreme Makeover*, while another comparable example would be the American show *The Swan*. The less aggressive makeover show *What Not to Wear* doesn't submit its victims to the ordeal of cosmetic surgery, but its premise is the same in that it can also be read as a metaphor for the panopticon. This is especially evident in the sequence where the 'prisoner' is placed in a mirrored box so that she sees her bottom reflected back at her (which certainly adds poignancy to the question 'does my bum look big in this?') and is therefore reminded that she is under constant surveillance.

Ten Years Younger is very emphatic that the woman is 'guilty' of various crimes against her body – such as sunbathing without protection or not moisturising her skin. The issue of 'guilt' is particularly interesting in relation to a make-over show such as this as the programme not only reminds women that they are inmates of the panopticon (patriarchal culture) but it also maps the make-over experience on to the ritual of religion – notably Christianity. Christian ritual revolves around the transformation of the emotion of shame into the more manageable emotion of guilt. Christianity is premised on the idea that we are all miserable, wretched sinners who should be ashamed of ourselves. In the Mass, Christians are required several times to acknowledge their shame and, prior to receiving communion, must even chant that 'we are not worthy so much as to gather up the crumbs under your table, oh Lord'. As various critics have explained (Connor 2001; Richardson 2004; Munt 2007) shame is a difficult emotion to cope with as it is very much a part of the self. As Munt argues, it has a sticky quality (2007: 12). We cannot separate ourselves from our shame as we are bound up in it. To feel shame is *to be* ashamed. In other words, shame refers to the self, to the person (see Connor 2001). Guilt, on the other hand, is a much more manageable emotion as it refers to specific actions. For example, in a court of law, the person pleads guilty to a specific crime. This person will then pay some sort of penance/penalty and then will no longer be guilty. He or she will have paid for his or her guilt and be absolved of it. One of the reasons (arguably) why Christianity is such an attractive religion is that it allows the subject to transcribe shame *into* guilt and then expunge that guilt. Through the act of confession we are able to transform this shame into the more manageable emotion of guilt and then 'pay' for this guilt with some form of Christian penance. It is this continuous transcription of shame into guilt which underpins most of the Christian calendar.

In many ways, a show like *Ten Years Younger* is offering the same ritual as can be found in Christianity. The woman is made to feel ashamed: by exhibiting her in the street and forcing her to hear the cruel comments from the passers-by, she feels shame. She *is* ashamed. However, the show allows her to transform this shame into guilt by giving her the chance to 'confess' her crimes of the past. The woman will confess that she has smoked too much; never exfoliated; never flossed her teeth; and sun-baked her poor skin without the all-important sun protection lotion. In other words, *Ten Years Younger* functions like Christian confession in which the person can turn the unbearable emotion of shame into the quantifiable actions of guilt. Then, just like Christian penance, the make-over victim must pay the price for her guilt – in the case of *Ten Years Younger* this is the gruelling ordeal of cosmetic surgery – and will then be deemed no longer guilty.

However, as already noted, the show *nearly* always uses a female body – although it has made a few attempts at male make-overs. One of the reasons why the male make-over is rarely a 'success' is, firstly, the question of narrative expectations. The moment of catharsis in this particular genre is when the tears of joy come as the 'victim' sees her transformed self. As a spectator, we like to see this visual cue, instructing us that this is a moment of jubilation – we may cry now too. Given patriarchal constraints, the male 'victims' rarely ever become teary eyed ('real' men don't cry according to the prevailing cultural scripts of gender) and so the narrative is an anticlimax. However, notwithstanding the question of narrative pathos, the issue does remain that men are not subject to the pressures of 'beauty' to the same extent that women are. One of the main examples of this is the issue of ageing. Men do not age any 'better' than women – in a biological sense – but *culturally* the signifiers of age are permitted, if not even respected or exalted, in men while they are denigrated in women. For example, a grey haired man is 'distinguished' while that adjective is usually not applied to a grey haired woman. (For key writing on ageing and femininity, see Wearing 2007, 2011.)

However, various critics have speculated that men are now subject to the tyranny of beauty as well (Bordo 1999). While there has certainly been some development in male self-consciousness about body image (see pp. 45–7 on metrosexuality), we agree with Kathy Davis who argues that 'I find it difficult to see men as the new victims of the "beauty myth"' (2002: 51). As Davis points out, this is evidenced in documentary representations which feature men submitting to the tyranny of beauty, especially cosmetic surgery. While women are represented as objects of pity, someone to feel sorry for, men are represented as eccentric, odd, if not even mentally unstable. The man who engages in cosmetic surgery is shown to be overly vain and someone who has more money than sense. The reason behind this is, quite simply, that men are not subject to the same tyranny of beauty-ism as women, so why would a man submit voluntarily to such gruelling ordeals?

However, the one exception to this is, arguably, gay men – especially those who live in a metropolitan setting. As we've argued already in Chapter 2, gay men are in the unique position of being both active pursuer but also object of the gaze. The very act of the gay 'cruise' (a gaze which not only registers sexual interest in another gay man but openly *inspects* that man's appearance) places gay men in a situation which is, to some extent, comparable to that of women. Most importantly, for contemporary gay men, the coming-out process is intrinsically linked to a self-appreciation of the body's appearance. This is because, in contrast to previous decades, more and more young gay men are coming out online. Often a young gay man's first contact with gay culture will be in the virtual reality of an online dating gallery such as Gaydar, Manhunt, Bigmuscle or Grindr. While this may be safer for young gay men than venturing into gay bars/clubs at the age of 18, the very mechanism of joining these sites requires a self-judgement of appearance, an interiorising of the gaze of gay culture. If we use Gaydar as an example, the gay man is requested to place a photograph of himself on the site. (He does not *need* to do this but he will soon learn that photo-less profiles receive very little attention.) The very act of taking the photograph (and the standard Gaydar profile shot is usually someone taking a self-portait on a mobile phone camera from a mirror reflection) forces the gay man to consider how his body is conforming to acceptable dictates of appearance in gay culture. Traditional Gaydar iconography, for example, dictates that the body should be represented shirtless, and so the man joining the gallery is forced to consider how his musculature will be appraised by the gaze of the other members. The website itself then performs further acts of policing as the profile requests that the gay man identify his body type from a range of options. He can either be 'slim', 'average', 'defined', 'muscular' or 'stocky'. As can be imagined, these are not equally weighted identifications as some carry much more desirability than others. This means that a young gay man must appraise his appearance, internalise the surveillance system and work out where he fits in the hierarchy of gay beauty. Gaydar itself then performs its most brutal act of panoptic policing when it runs its 'sex factor' competition in which the bodies represented on the site are *requested* to partake in a beauty pageant in which their bodies are ranked and judged by the other members of the dating gallery (for in depth analysis of Gaydar, see Mowlabocus 2010).

Given the similarity between the way gay male culture polices body image and the way patriarchal culture controls female body image, it is hardly surprising that the most popular make-over shows in recent years have been those in which the stylist/make-over expert is a gay man. In Chapter 2, we analysed the hugely popular *Queer Eye for the Straight Guy* which attempted to metrosexualise the make-over 'student', placing him in the position of gay man (both active, seducing subject and passive, appraised object) in order to police the body of a slightly slobby, down-at-heels, heterosexual man. However, one of the most hugely popular make-over gurus in recent years has been the gay identified Gok Wan who brought a new development to the make-over genre.

Wan is certainly a 'queer' subject, challenging many boundaries of identification: not least race and gender. He himself has joked about how his difference was often a great source of shame for him in his early days, stating that he was every bully's dream: he was fat, biracial and gay – the bully could take his pick. A key element in Wan's popularity is the fact that he was once overweight but, through diet and exercise, managed to slim down. He, therefore, in comparison to other make-over experts, offers a much more sympathetic form of guidance. His make-over strategy is always to tell the subject that he too knows what it is like to have body issues and low self-esteem and that he can help the person get over the problems as he did. Certainly, in comparison to the form of discipline exercised in shows such as *Ten Years Younger* or *What Not to Wear*, Wan's approach is premised on compassion rather than military style control.

The premise of Wan's most famous make-over show, *How to Look Good Naked*, is the same as *Ten Years Younger*. The make-over body is still reminded that she is an inmate in the panopticon, subject to the gaze of patriarchal culture. However, instead of standing the poor woman in the middle of the shopping centre, and asking for cruel and hurtful comments from passers-by, *How to Look Good Naked* projects a representation of the woman into a public space and the passers-by are asked to *compliment* the woman's body. Unlike *Ten Years Younger*, these passers-by are requested to address their comments directly to the woman and, without the anonymity of the video tape, the comments are always gracious. People will all focus on a 'beautiful' aspect of the woman's appearance ('she has a lovely smile'; 'she has a fantastic waist') rather than on negative aspects. All through this process, Wan is beside the woman and is continually complimenting her, reassuring her how beautiful she is and showering her with extreme gestures of physical affection.

The programme has another twist in its format in that the women is *not* required to undergo any form of body modification other than a new haircut. She certainly receives no surgical manipulation and any body modification is achieved purely through new, more figure 'flattering' clothes. Indeed, one of the most useful segments of the show (certainly for any spectator who is a high street shopper) is the one in which Wan takes the woman shopping and explains various techniques of dressing and styling the silhouette. For example, he might explain to the woman that wearing a broad belt gives the appearance of a narrower waist than a thin belt.

The next section of the show requires that the woman be photographed naked. This, of course, is not full nudity – occasionally there is a bare bum on display but little more than that – as the woman assumes the softly erotic pose traditionally found in glamour photography. This is always a professional photo-shoot, complete with make-up artist, flattering lighting and airbrushing to the final image. The woman is then shown this image and, of course, she is pleasantly surprised by how good she looks. The agenda of this activity is to reveal the constructed nature of images in fashion magazines. The woman is made aware that the reason these bodies look so *exceptionally* beautiful is because of the process of photography, make-up and airbrushing. Therefore, while still reminding the woman that she is an object of the patriarchal gaze, and should become a self-policing subject, *How to Look Good Naked* suggests that this gaze is not as oppressive as the other shows do. In many ways, this type of representation suggests one of the main sensibilities of post-feminism, which argues that an adherence to codes of feminine grooming need not be considered a constrictive aspect of femininity but something which women themselves may choose to enjoy and celebrate. A key tenet of post-feminism is that a feminist identification need not necessarily require a rejection of traditional feminine iconography (see Moseley 2002). Given the way that Wan continually 'strokes' the make-over subject, both her ego and, quite literally, when he cuddles and caresses her body, there is a suggestion that this is all affectionate and, most importantly, fun.

However, although *How to Look Good Naked* rejects the punitive nature of make-over shows such as *Ten Years Younger* and *What Not to Wear* (Gok Wan's women are never punished for their failures to adhere to conventional feminine iconography), the women are still subject to the patriarchal gaze, albeit in an ironic or playful fashion. It is here that the identification of Wan himself becomes important. As I suggested earlier, Wan is a queer subject in that his identification criss-crosses a number of boundaries. His class identification is ambiguous – is he working class or middle class? Similarly, his racial identification is obscure and difficult to classify. Most importantly, although he is a gay identified man, he is not the type of body that would be canonised in gay culture as supremely desirable. Therefore, when Wan makes-over the women, the issue of patronising these women is avoided. Where other make-over shows feature classically beautiful, upper-middle-class, white women, making-over women who are not only working class but also not necessarily classically beautiful, *How to Look Good Naked* features a queer body which, like his make-over subjects, is not conventionally beautiful.

However, the most interesting aspect of Wan's performance is the way he fluctuates between femininity (even overt effeminacy) and laddish masculinity. For example, his discourse may often contain, in the same sentence, terms which are associated with gay culture – 'fabulous' is one of his favourites – alongside phrases of laddish discourse to describe the woman's body parts. For example, the woman's breasts will often be referred to as 'bangers' or 'baps' before he proceeds to grab these breasts and (man) handle them in an utterly unapologetic way. It is here that the show offers a deliberate ambiguity. On the one hand, Wan is 'excused' this invasion of the woman's body because he is gay identified. Yet, on the other hand, we must remember that we are still watching a male body *man*handle a female body, haul her about the place, dress her, tell her what to wear, tell her how to act and, in short, treat her like a doll or a plaything. Therefore, although the show rejects the overtly punitive aspect of femininity that was seen in shows such as *Ten Years Younger*, it still reinforces patriarchal culture in which the female body is the object of the male gaze and represented on the screen as something for the male body to handle, *man*ipulate and play with.

6 Celebrity Bodies and Lifestyle Magazines

In this chapter we're going to be thinking about stardom and celebrity and why the study of it is useful for thinking about gender in the media, even though, for many people, the kind of knowledge we have about it isn't usually considered a legitimate academic pursuit but just trivial gossip or trash. However, many scholars have recently argued that, owing to the sheer ubiquity of celebrity discourse in popular culture, it is important to take the phenomenon seriously. In this chapter we will be focussing on something that celebrity discourse takes very seriously indeed: the body. One key development in gender studies has been the recent interest in the body image. While the body was once theorised as a given – something fixed and essential – we now view it as something which is constructed and regimented by culture. As we've seen already in the case of make-over TV shows, contemporary culture evidences an obsession with the regimentation of the body image, policing subjects into appropriate iconography. Looking at the body in celebrity culture provides an account of how meaning is generated around particular bodies and allows us to speculate on some of the significance of these meanings for the rest of us. Framing this chapter around 'celebrity culture' enables us to think carefully about the cultural, social and political context of particular versions of gendered identity, performance and the meanings generated around the body and to take very seriously this 'frivolous' aspect of popular culture. Before turning to the question of the body, however, it is worth thinking a little bit about the phenomenon of celebrity itself.

Celebrity Culture

We are all probably familiar with references to celebrity culture – which are often followed up by a comment on a decline in moral values. For example, in the summer of 2011 when large numbers of young people rioted in many cities in England following the fatal police shooting of

Mark Duggan in Tottenham in North London, some commentators referred to the rise of celebrity culture as part of the context for the looting and vandalism. So what does 'celebrity culture' mean and how can something which seems to be so 'trivial' also be held up as something with such serious political consequences? How should we begin to analyse such a widespread phenomenon? One useful definition of the multiple layers required to analyse the phenomenon of contemporary celebrity is offered by Graeme Turner:

> Celebrity is a genre of representation and a discursive effect; it is a commodity traded by the promotions, publicity and media industries that produce these representations and their effects and it is a cultural formation that has a social function.
>
> (Turner 2004: 9)

In terms of our readings of media in relation to gender, celebrity culture allows us to pay attention to the surrounding context; for example, by thinking about how stories of a particular celebrity, say Lady Gaga, Jennifer Aniston or David Beckham, might reflect the negotiation around changing definitions of appropriate gender performance, expectations and ideologies – dynamics which might include the construction of new modes of styling the body in terms of slenderness, class, gender ambiguity, masculinity and new versions of fatherhood and family. The magazine coverage of high profile celebrity couples, such as Wayne Rooney and his wife Colleen, Brad Pitt and Angelina Jolie, and David and Victoria Beckham, not only dissect minute variations of weight, mood, demeanour and behaviour but might also perhaps tell us something about the production and reproduction of gendered ideologies of the heterosexual family.

The point here is not to try to find out the 'real truth' about any given celebrity, which is, as critics have often pointed out, exactly what the writers of *Hello!* or *OK!* magazine purport to give us – the 'secrets of the stars'. Rather, the aim of this kind of work is to see what star and celebrity discourse can tell us about, as Richard Dyer puts it, 'how we are human now' (Dyer 2004: 15). What does the way that celebrities are marketed, venerated and/or 'trashed' say to us about contemporary relations between the sexes, negotiations of sexuality and identity, or ideologies of the family or the nation? Questions that theorists have asked about celebrity include asking about the processes involved in our relationship with it. Is our identification, or even antagonism towards it, an important aspect of our own identities? What is it that we are interested in, and what use do we make of the often copious and complex knowledge that we have of famous people?

Academic work on stars and celebrities comes from a number of starting points, including film studies, sociology, media studies and philosophy. Stars have, of course, nearly always been an important part of the Hollywood system. Once the initial excitement generated by the new technologies of the moving image wore off, interest quickly turned to the performers, building on the kinds of structures of fame already notable in vaudeville or the theatre. This fed into the system and actors were understood to be 'commodifiable' – able to be 'sold' as part of the product itself and, importantly, subject to a considerable amount of meta-discourse, which includes fan publications, scandal and publicity(de Cordova 1991; Butler 1998). The discipline of film studies has traditionally been more 'taken' (some might say obsessed) with the twin notions of the auteur (almost always the director) and genre as primarily important in understanding the way a film produces meaning, and has, historically, neglected the star as the significant site of meaning production. Needless to say this somewhat goes against the grain of actual movie going *practice* in the sense that while we might choose to see a film because of its director or genre we might also well be motivated by the industry's promotion of the star actors involved, such as when seeing a George Clooney film, a Kate Winslett film or a Robert Downey Jr Film (Butler 1998). The key theorist associated with 'stars' is Richard Dyer who utilises the semiotic notion of 'stars as texts' – indicating that they are fabricated and constructed by a range of processes and discourses. His work shows how stars perform ideological work – that is they convey meanings beyond the superficial. Diane Negra, in a study of stardom and white ethnicity in Hollywood, explains that:

> Stardom is one of the most devalued forms of social knowledge, yet it is a form of knowledge that we all possess, often with a high degree of expertise. Discourses on celebrities are capable of carrying a range of significant forms of information in regard to what we think we know about the world. What we say about stars is often a displaced form of discourse about our culture at large, and the belief systems that structure it.
>
> (Negra 2001: 8)

Negra reads stars or what she calls 'star personae' as 'cultural texts in which our understandings of gender, ethnicity and national identity are embedded' (ibid.: 9). What is seen to be at issue in the study of stars is the cultural weight they carry. Star 'texts' can be examined through the analysis of a variety of factors including the particular economic, ideological and psychological contexts which produce them and generate meanings around them.

Whilst recent discussion of celebrity and stardom have highlighted the pervasiveness of celebrity, it is important to recognise continuities with and differences from traditional conceptualisations of stardom. Hollywood's mode of production from the early part of the 20th century placed huge importance on the star as commodity – as well it might, given the investment made in the star. In what has been termed the classical period of Hollywood film, when the industry was dominated by large studios which controlled the production and distribution of the vast majority of films, stars were carefully managed and routinely 'plucked from obscurity' to become (potentially, if not in reality) the new golden boy or girl of the studio. The star's body, dress, hair, voice and frequently name too were 'made over' in the process of creating the persona. (For some of the more recent manifestations of this makeover logic, see Chapter 5.)

A compelling example is Marilyn Monroe. Strikingly, early photographs of Norma Jean Baker (as she was before her transformation), with long, mousy blonde hair, are almost unrecognisable as the iconic 'Marilyn' (in fact she looks much like the other starlets). Nevertheless they are also a key part of the 'text' of 'Marilyn Monroe', and one of the enduring stories is of her transformation from Norma Jean to Marilyn. While this is, of course, a very singular story – Monroe is a star whose image has remained extraordinarily potent some six decades after her death – it is also a very familiar and repeated story which is also true of many other stars and celebrities. For Dyer, this sort of example, points to one of the interesting ideological functions of celebrity in that the story of the rise to stardom helped to establish the democratic legitimacy of the process, since stars were emphasised as being 'like us' in their often humble origins yet also very decidedly 'not like us' in their lavish lifestyles (Dyer, 2004). This tension (ordinary versus extraordinary) is still very apparent in modern celebrity which has a very clear emphasis on consumption and aspirational lifestyle.

Another useful thing to notice here is that 'extra filmic' identity (the discourse around the star in terms of publicity, scandal, fan clubs, etc.), as well as that created across a range of film texts, is what makes up the star as a discursive phenomenon and which also stresses the fact that these are, so to speak, roles or stories which precede the individual who becomes the next James Dean, Clark Gable or Greta Garbo. Again, this is complex because, of course, the star is supposed to be a star by virtue of his or her extraordinary rather than ordinary characteristics. It is important for the 'myth' of stardom that *not* anybody can be a star; however, it is equally important that anybody might indeed have that potential – or to put it in today's context – might have the *X Factor*. It is clear, then, that the idea of 'manufactured celebrity', carefully orchestrated and managed, has a long history, although, as we shall go on to explore, the more recent rise of exceptionally short lived celebrity has taken this aspect of the star as a commodity, clearly manufactured and maximised for profit, to something of an extreme – Jedward, for example. There is a crucial economic dimension to the process of celebrity manufacture and dissemination, and it is a cultural phenomenon which employs a wide range of subsidiary roles and experts such as publicists, make-up artists, hairdressers and personal trainers. The role and reach of publicists in the control of access to celebrity, the 'celebrification' or 'celebritisation' of the public sphere and the role of the celebrity as a commodity which crosses (and sells) a range of media platforms all point to the importance of considering the political economy of the celebrity phenomenon.

Outside of the explicit production or manufacture of stars and celebrities, academics have looked at how star and celebrity stories reflect and engage with the particular cultural context in which they are located. For example, in very broad but important ways, stars can be understood to offer a promise of the rewards potentially on offer by capitalist culture for hard work and determination. This is particularly noticeable, for example, in the recent explosion of talent shows on television from *Fame Academy*, *Pop Stars* and *Britain's Got Talent* to *The X Factor* and *The Voice*. These shows all insist on the importance of an ethic of hard work for achieving the much coveted prize of eventual winner – despite the fact that this often coexists with an explicit set of discourses which emphasise the elusiveness of talent. Equally, the reality TV aspect of these sort of shows also demonstrate that in fact it's not hard work or effort or even talent but rather something very ordinary that can be turned into a short lived version of fame. In a broad sense this serves to mask the fact that social mobility is difficult to achieve and that very few people in modern mass mediatised societies ever achieve the kind of wealth and luxurious lifestyle of 'the stars'. Nonetheless, it remains a potent myth.

This is important for scholars interested in the social function of celebrity because it emphasises another aspect of the ordinary/extraordinary dynamic. For some scholars the expansion of the category of the celebrity into more and more related media outlets (from magazines and tabloids to the staples of television schedules) is a good thing – it is a 'democratisation' of the public sphere. Others argue that the 'ordinariness' of the reality TV participant or the talent show contestant is in fact a very particular construction of what it means to be ordinary and that the 'media ritual', to use Nick Couldry's term, participates in the production of what in fact turns out to count as 'ordinary' in a pattern which effectively produces the limits and boundaries of 'ordinariness' (Couldry 2003; Turner 2004). Even the painter and decorator who became a number one Christmas hit vocalist (Matt Cardell, winner of the 2010 *X Factor*) is recognisably 'ordinary', even at the moment of his apparent transformation. This serves effectively to obscure the 'hierarchical and exclusive' (ibid.: 83) nature of celebrity and the fact that very few are in a position to profit from it – certainly for any length of time.

Research has questioned the ways in which the cycle of producing celebrities via soap operas, talent shows and reality TV formats commoditises the (admittedly, apparently, very willing) participants in a cycle which is in fact driven by 'the pursuit of profit by large internationalised media conglomerates who ... still control the symbolic economy' (ibid.: 84). In this respect, the 'liberatory thesis' which suggests that the proliferation is in fact about democracy is thus shown to be rather limited. In turn this raises questions about the kind of damage that fame can do to those caught up in it. It also raises questions about the ways in which celebrities are 'consumed' by audiences both in terms of negotiating very real emotions, in spite of the distance between the consumer and the celebrity, and in terms of the everyday 'sadism' (Rose 2003) of our interest in seeing them 'knocked down'.

In keeping with the expansion of the traditional model of the star to encompass a wider range of fame, Chris Rojek has usefully (re)defined celebrity as 'the attribution of glamorous or notorious status to an individual within the public sphere' (Rojek 2001: 10). He goes on to qualify this because notoriety and glamour might often be thought of as mutually exclusive. For him the key is that they are linked by what he terms 'cultural impact' (ibid.); so 'celebrity' covers everyone from models to bombers. Rojek also suggests that we need to pay attention to who does the attributing – how are celebrities 'made'? He suggests that 'celebrities are cultural fabrications' (ibid.) who have cultural intermediaries – the legendary entourage or the industrial complex behind the facade (think here for instance about the ways that they are usually photographed surrounded by people). Celebrities are also defined by the fact that 'we' don't know them: 'social distance is the precondition for both celebrity and notoriety' (ibid.: 12).

Rojek also makes some useful distinctions between different kinds of celebrity. He identifies the first category as 'ascribed'. This form of celebrity is generally based on lineage or biological decent – e.g. Prince George, the most recent member of the British royal family, is predetermined to be a celebrity (like his father William or his uncle Harry, he can't help it). 'Achieved' celebrity, by contrast, describes celebrity status attained though perceived accomplishment: artistic talent or specialist achievements. Film stars, footballers and (some) musicians fall into this category: 'in the public realm they are recognised as individuals who possess rare talents or skills' (ibid.: 18). A third category is 'attributed', when this process is perceived to be based on intermediaries representing the individual in this way. The rise of the reality television celebrity is one example of this, though the category also includes people who become famous because of circumstances and then perhaps 'milk it' (often through the judicious use of publicists). There is no easy separation, however, amongst these different types of celebrity because publicity (like that surrounding starlets in the Hollywood system) has been an integral part of the commoditisation process for a long time. However, one of the understandings that things have indeed changed, and that the contemporary phenomenon of celebrity is somehow different from before, rests on these 'new' categories. At its most concentrated, Rojek calls this figure a 'celetoid', 'a media generated, compressed, concentrated form of attributed celebrity' (ibid.: 20). Rojek states that his objective is to achieve a more historical perspective and to widen the category from 'stars' and the entertainment business to include figures like the London nail bomber David Copeland. Rojek sees Copeland as an exemplar of the problems associated with the 'celebrity race' – which has such huge rewards of 'social recognition and belonging' for some whilst leaving most behind – and this is a culture which claims to recognise *all* as special and important. Rojek suggests that celebrity stalking and violent actions are explicable within 'celebrity culture' given the disparity between the cultural space occupied by 'celebrities' and that which the rest of us inhabit: 'some individuals transfer feelings of rejection and invalidation on to celebrities, who are regarded as representatives of social recognition and belonging, or externalize these feelings on to society at large for failing to recognize their special qualities' (ibid.: 147).

There is also an important economic dimension to celebrity which is big business, not only involving a wide range of distinct processes which literally construct the celebrity (fitness instructors, voice coaches, hairdressers, personal shoppers, agents, publicists, lawyers), but also because of the way the media industries have consolidated their businesses across a whole range of platforms. Celebrity can thus be understood as a recognisable 'brand' which can be utilised to sell entertainment products across a wide range of media. A simple example would be the use of *X Factor* stars to fill TV schedules but also to fill newspaper inches, to sell CDs and launch a thousand supermarkets. All this economic activity is one reason why the phenomenon of celebrity is currently taking the form that it does. Obviously, this is varied, and often understood as hierarchical (the familiar shorthand for this being the 'A' list, 'B list', etc.), but it is also specific to a particular industry (Marshall 1997). The music industry tends to produce celebrities with a different expected duration (despite some notable exceptions) than the film industry or the TV industry or those celebrified out of sporting achievement, though many academics have noted a distinct merging, even in these differentiated celebrities, making them in some cases more able to cross platforms. David Beckham, for example, was a football star, but his high profile marriage to another celebrity, the publicity surrounding their family and his numerous endorsements of fashion have expanded far beyond the original achievement to embrace a vast range of attributes which has in turn been heralded as offering new templates for masculinity in the early years of the 21st century. This brings us back of course to gender and the interest that celebrity holds for gender scholars.

Much of the discussion of contemporary celebrity makes clear that celebrities from different spheres need to be understood in their specificity – i.e. sports stars and film stars are created from quite different contexts, each of which carries very particular connotations; while celebrities from the music industry, television soap opera and reality programming follow quite different 'scripts'. Nonetheless, they do share, as Holmes and Redmond (2006) argue, 'the fame factor'. Attention then needs to be paid to the ways that modern celebrity media coverage, in some cases, tends towards the convergence of figures from different spheres as united by their celebrity status (and we'll return to this in our discussion of *Heat* magazine, see p. 107).

However, the differences between them are important for thinking about the potential significance of any given figure for addressing wider questions of social and cultural meaning – for our purposes, those meanings attaching to gender and sexuality in particular. To take a fairly random example, during the build up to the 2010 football world cup in

South Africa, the captain of the England football team, John Terry, was stripped of the role because of widespread coverage of his alleged affair with the ex-girlfriend of an England and one time Chelsea teammate. The 'married father of twins' transgression was considered serious enough to have professional implications for him, in part because of the nature of sporting celebrity and the role it plays in wider questions which, theorists argue, are intimately related to questions of the sociology and ideology of power. Chris Rojek suggest that sports celebrity, generally speaking, 'underlines the connection between self-discipline, training and material success' and so exemplary figures 'contribute to the dual ethic of individualism and personal competitiveness' (Rojek 2001: 37). David Marshall similarly suggests that we can understand celebrity as a 'system' which functions in distinct ways across a range of sites (his examples include film, television, music and politics) in which the mass media play an important role, governing the population via the organisation of 'affective power' (Marshall 1997: 243). Offering 'spectacular' versions of individuality, Marshall suggests that 'celebrities are *attempts* to contain the mass' (ibid.). Celebrity thus has a political function – it works to enhance the *value* of the individual and hence 'individuality'. Specifically, in the case of sports celebrity, Gary Whannel suggests that 'as the sporting star system has become central to the media sport industry, the images of sports stars become the point of convergence of social anxieties over morality and masculinity' (Whannel 2001: 1).

Therefore, to return to the story about John Terry, a gendered analysis would also want to consider more carefully the ways in which celebrity stories such as this one carry meanings which go beyond the 'role model' story (which after all is the whole point of his losing the captaincy). Instead, we might also want to explore the wider implications; for example, the meanings generated here in relation to the reification of heterosexuality and marriage (heteronormativity) and the way the story also draws attention to the symbolic function of women as objects of exchange between men (see Sedgwick 1985). In the UK context the widespread tabloid interest in the private lives of footballers, the phenomenon of the existence of a specific celebrity category the 'WAG' (wives and girlfriends), or just the existence of a shorthand 'footballers' wives' is worth unpacking more carefully for what it might tell us about how a particular, classed version of masculinity and femininity are produced through the circulation of stories of 'bad boy' footballers and their partners. Tellingly in this context, Owen Jones, in a book which challenges media depictions of the working class as 'chavs', singles out media coverage of working-class celebrities like Wayne Rooney, Cheryl Cole and, in a particularly striking and complicated case, Jade Goody (who became notorious for racist comments on the reality television show, *Celebrity Big Brother,* the non-celebrity version of which had made her a celebrity some years before), and points out that the vitriol levelled at them by the tabloid press about their lack of 'taste' and so on is part of a wider 'demonization' of the working class throughout the media (Jones 2011: 8). Gender plays a key role here as the stories of extramarital affairs, visits to prostitutes and so on speak to a drawing of boundaries around acceptable and unacceptable behaviour and what kinds of gender performance are deemed 'respectable'. Thus, whilst a certain amount of 'bad boy' behaviour would seem to be acceptable – a defining feature of being 'one of the lads' – there have been instances of stories of this behaviour leading to accusations of sexual coercion or even assault. Interestingly, the John Terry case highlights the importance of male bonding for the 'team spirit' of the England football team. A spirit that is jeopardised by the failure to conform to the unspoken, but nevertheless apparently well understood, codes of homosociality (Sedgwick 1985). Celebrity, then, sometimes seems to resolve a series of ideological conflicts that are socially or structurally based through a displacement on to the body of the star. Stars, Richard Dyer suggests, are 'embodiments of social categories' (Dyer 2004: 15) over which ideological issues, surrounding sexuality or race, for example, are contested. Relatedly:

> stars can function as sanctioned sites for ideological irruptions – that is, they can serve as comfortable cultural fictions for social realities. By distancing ourselves from the star through an understanding of that individual's extraordinariness, we can pleasurably partake in the meanings they are associated with, without having to directly confront questions of social relevance.
>
> (Negra 2001: 9)

For feminism, not surprisingly perhaps, star studies have held out very particular opportunities. Again at stake has often been the way that the bodies of stars negotiate meanings around gender and, as Negra demonstrates, ethnicity. In particular, focus has been on the way that the structures of the cinematic apparatus connotes woman (as something to be looked at); in particular the power of the gaze on the body of the woman and masculine desire. However, of crucial importance has also been the turn to actual audiences and their complex identifications with the star. In other words what might be seen to be at issue here is the very notion of subjectivity: *how* a star is recognised is as a fictional persona (despite our wanting to know the 'truth' of that person). An important intervention in the discussion of gender and stars comes from Jackie Stacey (1994). Stacey's argument is that the relationship between the stars and their audience brings up questions of the *audience's* subjectivity. Stacey provides an historical study of how women in the 1940s and 1950s in England used trips to the cinema and reading about Hollywood stars as important facets of their own lives, both through fantasies of escape and by an active effort to emulate. Her research emphasises that star personas are put to work by women not in a passive way but by an active engagement with the star's look and persona. This suggests that the relation between star and spectator is a complex negotiation which points to the construction of the self in relation to the other and the 'ordinary' ways in which identity and identification are practised in everyday life. This has vital theoretical significance too because, as Sue Thornham puts it:

> the concept of identification is here expanded from its use within psychoanalytic theory to become a more active and diverse process of negotiation. As such, it does not operate simply to confirm or fix existing gendered identities as psychoanalytic theory might suggest. It can also involve processes of transformation and the production of new, perhaps more contingent, partial and fragmented identities.
>
> (Thornham 1999: 164)

For some the role of the body in this process is less benign. Virginia Blum argues that 'surgical culture' is celebrity culture and vice versa. The visual culture we are bombarded with works through identificatory structures which take 'movie stars as paradigm'. The transformations of stars' bodies are explicitly coded in terms of the 'work' which produces them, though such transformations also offer up an idealised image which 'ordinary' bodies cannot hope to achieve without (and even, Blum's point is, *with*) surgery: 'after a century's worth of immersion in the close-up camera torture of star culture, we have come out the other side with the ferocious perspective of a cinematographer' (Blum 2003: 264). This ferocious perspective is also often sadistic, as she notes in her analysis of the way that discourses around stars often viciously reverse the transformation – by 'exposing' or 'outing' them as surgical subjects and also never failing to point out what more 'needs' doing.

However, the surgically enhanced celebrity body can also be read as offering a transformatory potential in that the obviously modified body exceeds the limits of feminine beauty as set by the normative constraints of 'surgical culture'. Diane Negra (2001), for example, argues that Cher, whose surgically enhanced body has made her the butt of many jokes, nonetheless also exceeds this framing, becoming a scandalous and subversive body. In other words, Cher's surgically modified body calls attention to the work *expected* of female bodies: 'the bodily impossibility she represents is equivalent to the impossible position of all women's bodies under late capitalism. In its refusal to be assimilated, safely commodified, and stable, Cher's "impossible" body displays a subversive level of knowledge about the cultural work women's bodies are expected to perform' (ibid.: 178). Interestingly this is an argument which can also be made in relation to the recent phenomenon of celebrity magazines, which revel in demonstrating just how hard celebrities have to work to maintain their bodies. Often they 'fail', generating debates in the process such as, for example, 'how thin is too thin?', which some see as potentially helpful in a climate where the 'tyranny of slenderness' (Bartky 1990) holds such general sway.

Celebrity Magazines: The Couple and the Bikini

A cursory glance at a range of UK celebrity magazines is enough to reveal three key preoccupations: the 'couple'; the scrutiny of the female body (for signs of weight loss or gain, measurement of muscle versus 'curves', dress size); and how to achieve a celebrity look in the high street. Interestingly, the first two preoccupations are often linked since the celebrity's body is often offered as a symptom of her marital or relationship difficulties. In this section, we want to look very briefly at a few of these articles to get a snapshot of celebrity magazine culture and to speculate on the importance that coverage of celebrity in magazines has for thinking about gender in the media. As we have seen in the first part of this chapter, the term celebrity covers a very wide range of bodies, and the magazines that we are going to refer to here also range from the celebrity-friendly *Hello!* to the upmarket *Vanity Fair* to the gossip oriented *Closer* and *heat*. These magazines, as we would expect, deploy very different modes of address to the reader. From *Vanity Fair*'s more 'serious' approach to politics and current affairs (which by no means disqualify it from being completely immersed in celebrity) to

Hello!, which showcases the homes of the famous and gives them the opportunity to present themselves apparently as they see fit (the magazine is notorious for its sycophancy), to *heat*, whose signature shot is the grainy long lens of the paparazzi (or even the reader's mobile phone). *heat*'s province, as Su Holmes puts it, is 'the playing out of how the public visibility of celebrity now saturates the everyday ... this is the rhetoric of "unkempt and unready": the unflattering snap of the celebrity sunbathing on holiday, eating lunch in a cafe or walking home drunk from a night out' (Holmes 2005: 24). Holmes is careful to distance this kind of everyday exposé from the more traditional type of celebrity exposé stories, to which, of course, it is nonetheless discursively related. This is, in part, as Holmes points out, because *heat*, like *Hello!* but with a more ambivalent and perhaps more incoherent agenda, is dependent on 'the cooperation of the celebrities themselves' (ibid.). This leads to a very particular working through of the ordinary/extraordinary dynamic that we saw earlier, owing to the mutual reliance of stories about reality TV, soap opera and the rise of the apparently 'ordinary' celebrity which makes up the majority of *heat*'s coverage.

In relation to gender and *heat* magazine, one of the first points to make would be to think about how and whether it is aimed at a primarily female reader. One obvious but key point to make here would be the long history of women's magazine publishing which has historically included exemplary or exceptional figures as part of their content and the continuity with these magazines as well as the differences. Much of the academic interest in magazines has centred on their mode of address to women – the intimate, gossipy tone which draws the reader in as part of a shared knowledge community. This kind of knowledge is culturally denigrated and dismissed. In a key argument about women's magazines, Joke Hermes suggests that, although the use of magazines may often be experienced as 'meaningless', with some of the respondents of her ethnographic study unable to recall much about what they had read, readers did draw on the content in everyday ways through empathy and identification as well as occasional anger and frustration. However, for a number of critics, women's magazines are culpable in their relentless emphasis on shopping, consumption and the quest for the ideal body, which make them powerful ideological mediators and as such worthy of critical attention (Bordo 2003). In a recent article about *heat* magazine, however, Rebecca Feasey argues that the magazine *may* be read as a 'potentially empowering discourse for female readers' in that it offers validation of 'feminine competencies' and offers 'positive frames of reference' (Feasey 2006: 178, 180) for the reader who is able not only to imitate celebrity shopping habits at a knock-down price but also to see the 'beauty myth' under construction and to witness the difficulty rather than the flawless perfection of celebrities who are routinely shown in less than flattering photographs.

Women's magazines have also been understood to perform an important role in the construction and fabrication of femininity – often with some competing paradigms within the pages of the same magazine – so that femininity can primarily be understood through discourses of domesticity and motherhood *or* glamour and fashion. In recent media discourse the figure of the 'yummy mummy' – very much staged in relation to celebrity culture, with Victoria Beckham, Gwyneth Paltrow and Katie Holmes being cases in point – seem to wed these, historically somewhat diverse, aspects of femininity together. Again, however, it is important to recognise some continuity, as well as distinctiveness, in this kind of coverage, since in general terms 'stars' are partly understood *as* stars precisely when their private, family life is as much in play as their public role. Nonetheless, a very particular contemporary inflection seems apparent in the way that coverage of celebrity women, who have recently given birth, obsessively follows the celebrity's 'battle' to 'lose the baby fat' and return to a pre-pregnancy size within a few weeks of giving birth – a feat which most 'ordinary' women, without the help of a personal trainer, a nanny to watch the baby while you exercise or, it should be said, the expectations of the celebrity press following you around and checking on your 'progress', find rather more difficult to achieve. Again, Blum's work is helpful here for thinking about the ways in which this kind of 'exemplary' embodiment may have quite serious possible psychological consequences for the young mother whose body hasn't returned to its pre-pregnancy size within weeks of giving birth. This kind of exemplary embodiment, which is venerated by the celebrity press, thus might then allow us to think about the potential consequences of such public performances of maternity.

However, celebrity coverage of maternity and maternal subjectivity hasn't always been read in such negative terms. For example, Imogen Tyler's exploration of pregnant female subjectivity takes as its starting point a famous *Vanity Fair* photograph of a heavily pregnant Demi Moore to suggest that celebrity in this case violates an extremely important taboo surrounding the possibilities for imaging and imagining 'a pregnant subjectivity':

The taboo breaking publication of the Moore photograph ... presents the possibility to address the absence of the pregnant subject within existing theoretical frameworks and to begin to imagine her presence. The photograph can thus be read as a shield against the imaging of foetal personhood and a refusal of the mother/child dichotomy that monopolises discourses around reproduction.

(Tyler 2001: 81)

In this case, 'celebrity' enables a rethinking of identities, although it's also important to note that the foetus in this argument is also celebrified 'in the public sphere of "super personhood", where it radiates authenticity and elicits strong identification' (Lauren Berlant cited in ibid:81), and so celebrity then is deployed in perhaps contradictory ways but with notable effects.

To return to *heat* magazine, however, the emphasis that it puts on the body of the celebrity is another somewhat contradictory discourse in that even at the point that it appears to celebrate the 'liberation' from the tyranny of slenderness it also reconfirms it in the most obvious way. An example comes from the 20–26 August 2011 issue. The cover story is 'Don't Make Us Diet' in which stars rebel against the pressures of fame and pictures are offered of four celebrities in bikinis on holiday all of whom are apparently 'rebelling' against the constraints of celebrity thinness. All are 'quoted' as saying 'I'm a normal girl – I love food' (Stacey Solomon: 'I'm fed up with trying to be perfect'; Sarah Harding: 'I've never counted calories so I'm not starting now'). (Fernando and Barrett, 2011, cover story)

Many critics have seen the ways that women are encouraged to mould their bodies in accordance with a range of 'disciplinary practices' (Bartky 1988) which encourages a mode of constant self-surveillance and operates in a worrying relation to conditions such as anorexia nervosa and bulimia (Bordo 2003). At first sight then this might look like a progressive and even helpful injunction, but it is worth noting that alongside the text are the pictures which are presented ('first bikini pics!') in such a way as to make a spectacle of the celebrities' bodies and which encourages the viewer to evaluate the 'curves' and to judge whether or not the celebrity has gained weight. It is the midriff and the breasts that are particularly on show here. This invitation to dissect and judge is even more apparent in the picture which is not part of the story but which is linked to it through the motif of the bikini. For example, a picture of Coleen Rooney will have an arrow pointing to her stomach and the caption 'food baby or real baby?' (Fernando and Barrett, 2011, cover). Inside the magazine the story continues with vital statistics given alongside 'before and after' imagery of all the cover celebrities. So, whilst the story itself is one of apparent resistance (they are labelled 'diet rebels'), the pictures tell a more ambivalent story, particularly as the 'before' pictures are frequently more 'posed' and professional that the 'off guard, unkempt, unready' (Holmes 2005) 'after' shots. Another point to bear in mind in this story is that men are by no means exempt. Indeed, the cover of this particular issue also has a photograph of David Beckham, looking a bit portly, with the caption 'Nooo! Becks has got a beer belly!'. The 'inside story' on Beckham, however, is a far cry from the female celebrities, for whom career expectations or relationship problems are held accountable for their relationship to food. Instead the story of Beckham has a larger version of the cover shot, but this time with arrows pointing to his 'belly' and 'bulge', the commentary far from revealing any anxiety about his emotional or professional health. Instead there is offered a jokey objectification of the footballer under the headline 'Who's a Big Boy then Becks?': 'To say we did a double-take is a lie. We've studied these pictures at least 783 times in an hour spending equal time trying to get our head around Beck's belly and staring at his package' (Croners, *heat*, 20–26 August 2011, p. 23). So whilst certainly not exempt from *heat*'s particular brand of celebrity body bashing, nonetheless there are distinctions in the ways that the male body is presented as 'faulty' even when it apparently shares the same kinds of surveillance and ridicule.

Celebrity discourses, then, allow us to think about the way that male and female bodies are both constructed and consumed in popular culture and at how changing templates for masculinities and femininities are disseminated so as to be picked over, hated or adored. Such picking is described by psychoanalytically oriented critics as sadistic and narcissistic and a licence for 'curiosity at its most ruthless' to be given (almost free) reign (Rose 2003). It is not surprising then that so many celebrities seem to resent and resist the 'intrusion' of the public into their 'private' lives. This, as Jacqueline Rose argues, is in fact key to the performance of celebrity, since celebrities are most 'celebrity like' when they openly resist the public's desire to 'annul the mystery' of their celebrity. Recent developments in social media such as Twitter might appear to disrupt this since being able to 'follow' the celebrity seems to speak to a dispelling of the distance between 'us' and 'them'. But perhaps the questions should be asked the other way round. How is it that Twitter so quickly became associated with the ever expanding domain of the celebrity?

The next chapter takes us into the intriguing debates of how gender is represented and negotiated within the digital world of online communities, chat rooms, dating galleries and new media platforms such as Twitter and Facebook.

7 New Media and 'Performing' Gender: Online Dating

As the previous chapters have stressed, media representations are extremely important in negotiating questions of identity in relation to sexuality, class, race, ethnicity and, of course, gender. The ideas which we have about ourselves do not just 'happen' by accident but are shaped and transformed through our cultural and material experiences and in relation to the (media) discourses which surround us. Media representations are highly influential in shaping identifications in various ways and these can range from issues of fashion and consumption to influencing social prejudices such as misogyny, racism and homophobia.

However, in all the earlier chapters we have considered the politics of representations within 'authored' media texts – in other words, texts that are completed by the production company and then distributed for consumption. The spectators negotiate the representations and interpret their meaning. As we have argued, there is no 'postal service' of meaning since a spectator's interpretation of a text will depend as much upon his or her own identifications (class, race, gender, generation, etc.) and media literacy as it will upon how the text is coded. Nevertheless, hegemonic ideologies are in circulation throughout the dominant media and discourses of gender/race/class/sexuality are encoded throughout popular culture.

In this chapter we will consider the politics of an interactive media text in which the spectator becomes a participant. Unlike film, television or print media, online media texts – such as chatrooms or dating galleries – allow the spectator to become a participant and engage in the construction of personal identification through mediated relations with other participants. While the traditional forms of mass media might loosely be described as 'top down' and, from a critical gender perspective, may represent hegemonic identifications to the spectator, the internet permits the spectator a framework for active participation and engagement with media content and thus arguably produces a different kind of negotiation of subjectivity and identification (Ferreday 2009; Mendelson and Papacharissi 2011; Mandiberg 2012). Scholars describe this distinctive form of engagement, with the new conditions of media environments, in terms such as 'convergence culture', 'participatory culture' and 'user generated content' (Mandiberg 2012). All of this suggests real shifts in the power dynamics of how content and individuals interact. In this chapter we introduce some of the questions around gender that this media environment produces. For example, do online chatrooms offer the potential of a post-gender utopia in which the limiting binary of gender is queered or completely overthrown? Or do these texts simply reinforce hegemonic ideologies of gender scripts comparable to any other example from popular culture? Or is the answer likely to be somewhere in between these positions?

Gender Online

The World Wide Web is still a relatively youthful media – approximately 20 years old. (Although internet exchanges, such as emails, were established in the 1970s, via military and university network systems, the World Wide Web was not created until the 1990s.) Scholarship of online and digital technology has expanded greatly over the past decade and there are now university courses devoted to the study of digital and Web technology. Traditionally, as many have noted, the arguments about the Web have been somewhat polarised into the optimistic utopian strand of 'new media, new possibilities' rhetoric or a pessimistic vision of the internet as the lair of crime, degradation, rampant commercialisation and, perhaps the most current discursive concern, as the haunt of the paedophile. This stark polarisation has also been notable in debates over the gender politics of online engagements. However, most in depth studies reveal the much more nuanced picture of online environments, offering both spaces for self-definition and agency but also environments in which gender politics are sometimes far from progressive (Karlsson 2007; Attwood 2009; Taylor 2011; Nakamura 2012).

In this chapter we will outline three main developments in the study of online, interactive media and gender politics. First, we start with the earliest scholarship which praised internet forums and virtual worlds for its liberatory potential, and which welcomed the possibility of effacing gender through new dynamics of interaction. Second, we trace the development of these debates, which questioned how often online media texts were actually subverting or transforming gender and which

considered the moral and ethical issues surrounding internet performance. Third, we consider some of the more recent turns in academia
which have argued that, far from encouraging gender fluidity, online
spaces often reaffirm hegemonic gender ideologies and police these in a
highly restrictive fashion. We will finish with some thoughts on recent
events concerning cyberbullying and trolling and how these practices
appear to be new forums for sexism and misogyny.

The Internet as a Blank Canvas for New Identifications

The earliest feminist scholarship on the internet saw a great potential in
online representations to move beyond the limiting sex–gender–sexuality continuum of hegemonic culture (Turkle 1995; Poster 1995).
Removed from the body (often referred to as the 'meat' by internet
fans), an online text, such as a chatroom or other interactive program,
provided a potential platform for exploring/creating new identifications
in relation to class, sexuality, race and gender. As Foster points out,
'both text-based and graphical virtual interfaces make possible the
decoupling of public persona from the physical space of the body'
(Foster 2001: 440) and so a participant in an online chatroom may
claim an identification that is different from the one he or she maintains in everyday life. In this respect, these online texts, arguably, offer
the potential to efface cultural identifications such as race, ethnicity,
class and gender. An internet chatroom may be viewed as offering a
blank canvas in which the participant can build his or her own identifications removed from the confines of everyday discourses. A chatroom
user might identify as a different class, sexuality, race or gender, or even,
within some fantasy spaces, as something non-human such as a myth-
ical creature or warrior. In this respect, critics such as Turkle read the
internet as exemplary of postmodernism with its emphasis on fractured
and multiple identifications. Turkle argues that 'the Internet is another
element of computer culture that has contributed to thinking about
identity as multiplicity. On it, people are able to build a self by cycling
through many selves' (1995: 178). Most importantly, an online interactive text allows us the possibility of revealing only the aspects of our
identifications that we wish to reveal to other users. There is no requirement to reveal physical age, race or gender. As Rheingold points out,
'because we cannot see one another in cyberspace, gender, age, national
origin, and physical appearance are not apparent unless a person wants
to make such characteristics public' (Rheingold 1993: 26).

In a similar vein, the internet gives us the possibility to foreground or inhabit whatever aspect of our identification we want to inhabit at that particular time. In the same way that we inhabit different identities appropriate for different contexts and times (the identity a student has in a university seminar will probably be very different from the one he or she performs in a nightclub on Saturday night) so the internet also allows us a faster and more convenient way of shifting in and out of identifications at different times. Indeed, given the mobility of new technology, someone could shift identifications in a matter of minutes. For example, a student may well be performing the identity of 'serious scholar' in the context of a lecture but may then leave the lecture theatre and log on to an internet chatroom on his or her mobile phone where he or she will assume the online persona of 'sex-o-holic' and have hardcore text-sex with another online user – while sitting in the university cafeteria sipping a low-fat latte. Such a blurring of identifications is facilitated by the internet and new mobile technology in a way that was not possible for previous generations.

While some online fantasy identifications are simply fantasies – a person plays an online sword & sorcery game for a few hours and/or engages in cyberchat or cybersex in a chatroom and then returns to everyday life – there are other sites which request that users take their online identifications much more seriously. Dahlberg, for example, argues that there are two genres of online, interactive texts: 'sites of "authentic fantasy" online ... can be differentiated from sites of "real authenticity". That is, sites where the intention is to "perform" can be distinguished from sites where the intention is to "be"' (Dahlberg 2001: 89). For example, a person performing a warrior god in an interactive fantasy game is a different identification from someone chatting in an online dating chatroom or social media network where the intention may well be to meet up with someone in real life in order to pursue some sort of romantic relationship or friendship. For example, Facebook has been considered by Mendelson and Papacharissi (2011) who have argued that there is little experimentation taking place but instead the photographs uploaded on to the site serve the function of producing a type of online autobiography. Their analysis suggests, however, that the contours for this are in fact highly circumscribed. In their study of college students they note that the construction of identity is surprisingly uniform: 'the commonality of the images within each student's collection, and between all the students, demonstrates that, while the outfits and locations change, the types of events documented and the nature of the poses do not. The same stories are told and retold in these photographs' (ibid.: 267). In their study they conclude that the photographs work to construct both identity and importantly a shared experience: 'they validate the sense of a *real* college experience. Facebook pictures are where college students visually play out their lives for each other ... These practices serve as performative exercises of identity and belonging, simultaneously declaring and corroborating shared experience' (ibid.: 270). In this view, social media are seen as sites which are embedded in the construction of self and identity.

However, this distinction between the sites where the users 'perform' as opposed to sites where they want 'to be' may not be as clear for all online participants. For many people, who spend long periods of time engaging in online interactions, their alter ego may well be more 'real' to them than their physical self. If the most meaningful interactions that a person has occur in the context of an internet chatroom or a sword & sorcery game, who is to say what is more 'real' for that participant? In this respect, much early online scholarship noted the potential for viewing the digital world as the supreme example of Baudrillard's (1983) thesis of hyper-reality in which representation is now more 'real' than reality. Perhaps somebody despises his or her everyday existence and 'lives' for the times that he or she can in the virtual online world in which his or her alter ego leads a much more interesting life. Indeed, the pleasure of online virtual reality worlds – the most famous is probably Second Life – allow participants to forge alternative realities for themselves through their online avatar.

Cross-gender or cross-race identification, in this context, could have enormous benefits in increasing a person's awareness and sensitivity to others (Bruckman 1992; Danet, 1998, Turkle 1995). Experiencing what it is like to be gendered or raced as an other should, it is suggested, lead to greater awareness of minority communities and give an understanding of how 'the other half lives'. In a similar vein, if an online forum can reduce race/gender/class to a simple linguistic identification (changing gender is only a few taps of the keyboard and a couple of mouse-clicks away) then why are we so concerned with these identifications in the real world? Demonstrating that identifications are simply a matter of performance can de-essentialise these identifications for the participant and promote an implicit understanding of how these identificatory regimes function in contemporary culture.

However, more recent scholarship has considered whether 'cross' identifications are actually happening in online interactions and, if they are happening, exactly how well they are succeeding. For example, Rellstab (2007) and Kendall (1998) both performed qualitative analysis on a range of online chatrooms and discovered that there were problems with cross-gender identifications in these forums. Kendall argues that '"switching" genders leads many to perform exaggerated and easily unmasked caricatures' (1998: 140). A man performing femininity in an online forum does not always 'pass' very well as female as he may be representing clichéd, caricatured or even stereotyped expressions of femininity. Often, many cross-gender male participants may perform a pneumatic cartoon of an idealised woman (the equivalent of a schoolboy's erotic doodle), which is immediately read by other participants as fake.

This commonplace failure of cross-gender identifications in online chatrooms, in which male participants fail to perform convincing expressions of femininity, is arguably due to the fact that gender is experienced. We learn how to perform masculinity and femininity through everyday cultural discourses and unlearning or undoing these iterative practices is difficult. As Herring and Martinson point out, 'conventionally gendered ways of communicating are deeply embedded in people's social identities' (2004: 443–4) and so these differences are difficult to unwrite – even in chatroom conversations. Therefore, the inability to perform or pass as the opposite gender may suggest a completely different set of politics to the participant. Instead of the internet offering new possibilities of moving beyond the gender binary, chatrooms may actually have the opposite effect and reinforce essentialist ideas of gender. For example, if a male participant tries to pass as female in a virtual world but fails miserably – and is 'outed' and banned from the chatroom by the other users – this can reinforce the notion that gender is fixed and cannot be twisted or transcended. In this respect, cross-gender identifications online, which fail and are 'outed' by the other participants, may be similar to low-brow drag acts in which the performer is very obviously a man in women's clothes and therefore reinforcing the notion of gender essentialism. A failure to pass as the opposite gender online potentially reinforces a sense of gender fixity rather than fluidity for the participants.

Moral and Ethical Issues of Performing Online Identifications

Related to the idea of cross-gender identification in online worlds and chatrooms is the ethical issue of whether someone *should* attempt to identify as the opposite gender given that the question of deceiving other participants is at stake. Obviously, this is a thorny issue and there are various different arguments in the equation. On the one hand, there is the genuinely disconcerting issue that many online participants might well be children (or naïve adults) who genuinely believe everything they read from their online 'buddy'. What if this young child is communicating with someone she believes to be another girl of her own age when, in reality, she is in communication with a 50-year-old man? What if the discussion moves from dolls and television cartoons to sexualised topics? What if the young child's new internet friend suggests that they meet up in person? Obviously the very real dangers of online communication, when one participant is misrepresenting him or herself, *cannot* be overestimated, and tragic high profile recent cases of children being coerced into sexual activity, blackmailed by impersonators and even driven to suicide are a reminder of the reality of these dangers. A 2013 report by the Child Exploitation and Online Protection Centre (CEOP) in the UK highlights the links between the opportunities offered to children to experiment with identity and the vulnerability that this places them in when online:

> The internet also offers children the opportunity for a separate identity in which they can be whoever they wish and take risks they would never countenance offline. It is often where these two worlds meet that children suffer most at the hands of those wishing to do them harm. That a child's internet presence is now so inextricably linked to their real world identity can only increase the impact of any exploitation they suffer.
>
> (CEOP 2013)

Recent research into what worries children themselves online has shown that it is content – in particular, pornography and violence (the top two risks identified) and that they are distressed by encountering it. However, the risk depends on the different platforms, and so websites and video sharing are linked to anxieties experienced by children over pornography and violence, though the report suggests that 'chatrooms are mostly connected to contact related risks (43%) and to conduct-related risks (27% of all risks linked to chatrooms)' (Livingstone et al. 2013: 7). Further, although the figures for children's perception of contact-related risk associated with 'people pretending to be someone else' were quite low at 1.8% of all risk compared with 5.6% for 'inappropriate contact in general' and 3.2% for 'the possibility of inappropriate contact in general' (ibid.: 7), the figures do show that children are themselves concerned about the online environment.

Yet, and without detracting from the very real dangers flagged by these reports, we can also read chatroom conversations or virtual world interactions in a rather different light as a postmodern brand of 'story-telling' or role playing. As the CEOP report acknowledges, these can be interactive texts allowing *willing* participants to invent and narrate their own stories, and so a chatroom participant can be an online author. It is a standard joke about chatrooms that many of its participants are engaging in fantasy masquerades in which their online personas have the appearance of supermodels while, in reality, the participants are extremely unattractive people. However, these are people who are simply enjoying the opportunity that the internet gives them to escape the confines of their everyday identifications: identifications which, presumably, are not very happy ones. In many ways, this is simple story-telling; two people who are inventing narratives to give them a little pleasure, a little diversion, on a lonely, boring winter's night. Like all fiction texts or entertainments, the participants are engaging in a willing suspension of disbelief in which they immerse themselves in the fantasy world of their erotic sagas to provide a pleasurable diversion on a dull evening. Internet chatrooms have been particularly enjoyable for people who have extreme sexual desires. For example, people who are into feeder fantasies (obtaining sexual pleasure from feeding and fattening-up a partner) may well not indulge these desires in their everyday life but may occasionally log into a chatroom devoted to this particular fetish so as to live out and explore their fantasy with other willing participants (see Richardson 2010). Arguably, this is all simple 'play', and to draw equations between the fantasies people enact online and what they do in everyday life is very reductive.

However, while there may well be some internet forums/chatrooms which cater for alternative sexual desires, the majority of 'romantic' internet sites (for example, chatrooms and dating forums) do not seem to be striving for alternative representations of the self but for the most hegemonic ones. This leads us to a third development in scholarship on internet sites and gender identification: the importance of online media in reinforcing hegemonic ideals of gender and the body.

Queering Gender Online: Critical Fantasy or Common Practice?

Recent scholarship has pointed out that, far from effacing the tyranny of hegemonic culture and creating a gender-fluid utopia, the internet is actually reinforcing hegemonic, conservative ideas of masculinity and femininity. In addition to the exclusions many face in accessing and participating in specific online activities and the cultures of gender that are thereby reinforced, the internet is also a site for the reification of body tropes associated with hegemonic versions of both masculinity and femininity.

As we've argued in the previous section, it is a standard joke that, in chatrooms and virtual worlds, the internet user's body does not match his or her online representation. If someone, for example, is a little plump then he or she usually makes his or her avatar a little more svelte. However, we have to wonder if the opposite is ever likely to happen? Are there examples of people making their avatars fatter or shorter – in other words images that correspond less to hegemonic regimes of masculinity and femininity?

Of course, the above example is from an online fantasy world in which the user is, arguably, enjoying the chance to escape from issues which he does not like in his own personal life. In that respect, perhaps his avatar is also richer and has a better, more satisfying job than the user does in his real life? Yet, this issue of reinforcing hegemonic ideals of gender is also visible in sites which aim for representational authenticity such as dating galleries – in which the stated goal is to use the gallery as a platform from which to meet someone in real life.

For example, if someone joins an online dating gallery, that person is required to fill out an online form which details the person's physical and emotional characteristics. The problem is that the options which a person can select on this form have a limited number of choices – not least in relation to body type. As we all know, the majority of bodies do not fit into narrow definitions such as 'athletic' or 'muscular' – and these terms are notoriously difficult to quantify– and so most bodies are simply left the option of selecting the rather uninspiring identification tab of 'average'. The other alternatives are probably 'slim' or 'stocky' – in other words euphemisms for the dreaded 'skinny' or the even more knee-shaking terror of 'fat' – one of the most feared words in contemporary culture (see Richardson 2010). In this respect, a participant in an online dating gallery has only a very few – and very conservative – identifications to claim in relation to body type. The result of this tyranny is that there are a great many people who are identifying online as 'athletic' or 'muscular' – given that the other alternatives are the shameful and undesirable identifications. (Who wants to identify as 'average'?) Therefore, it's hardly surprising that many online participants are stretching the truth a little when it comes to their gallery identifications.

The other key point to remember about this sort of interactive text is that it forces the participant to become aware of his or her body image and gender performance. An online dating gallery demands that the participant appraise his or her body image and gender performance and make auto-evaluative judgements about themselves. Perhaps the participant had never really considered whether he or she were 'average', 'athletic' or 'stocky' but is now required to do so if he or she wishes to participate in the online dating forum.

One of the most 'body fascist' of contemporary internet dating sites has been the (relatively) long established gay dating site Gaydar. Recently this site was the subject of sustained investigation by Sharif Mowlabocus whose superb book *Gaydar Culture* (2010) analysed the politics of identification in relation to this site. One of the important political issues to stress in relation to this site is that more and more young gay men are coming out online. For a number of these men, their first gay interaction is in the context of an online dating chatroom or forum. While this is certainly a safer coming-out process for young gay men than, say, public park cruising (as would have happened several decades ago) it does force young men to appraise their body image and gender performance in a fashion that may not have been the case in a different context. For example, not only does Gaydar require that the user identify his body type from the narrow menu of 'athletic', 'muscular', 'slim' (read 'skinny') or 'stocky' (read 'fat') but it also asks that the penis size be identified from yet another equally limiting list of 'small', 'average', 'large' or 'extra large'. The important thing to stress is that there is no technical quantification here. What exactly is an 'extra large' penis? Indeed, for somebody in the process of coming out for the first time, who may not have encountered many (erect) penises before, the only source of comparison will be the easily obtainable representations of online pornography. The chance of finding penises in porn which are not 'extra large' will be rather rare and so porn-penises may well be the litmus test against which online participants judge their own manhood. The result is that there are probably a great many people who are either shamefully identifying online as being 'small' (when, relative to the majority, they are average) or are lying and identifying as 'extra large' because it seems to be the only thing that is represented as desirable and, of course, so many other profiles seem to identify with it. Although Gaydar is an extreme example, the phenomenon of 'internet penis size' is well known and is yet another standard joke about online culture.

Remaining with Gaydar as a textual example, it's also interesting to note how the site polices gender performance in a fashion which is extremely troubling. While racist comments are quite rightly not permitted on the site, and the user will be asked to delete them from his profile, effeminophobic comments are not subject to the same adjudication. Of course, we are not suggesting that people are not allowed to express an erotic preference, and if someone writes 'I am only interested in masculine, straight-acting men' he is simply asserting his personal taste. However, what is interesting about the site is the way many profiles don't simply stop at announcing their own personal taste but continue to attack savagely men whose gender performance violates traditional notions of the masculine. Below are some examples of the comments made in various users' profiles, asserting not simply hatred but *disgust* for men who challenge the gender binary:

> Effeminate men make me sick.
> I only like men who are men. If you are a man who thinks he is a woman then that is just wrong. Do not message me.
> I don't like girlie men. Do not message me if you flap your hands in a girlie way; talk with an effeminate lisp; cross your legs when you sit down. You must not go swishing [moving in an effeminate manner] down the road or mincing along the street.

The last comment on a user's profile really expresses the way the site allows participants to police normative gender. Apart from the fact that this user believes there is a quantifiable difference between 'swishing down the road' and 'mincing along the street' (a somewhat specious distinction, in our view) it does express the sense of disgust when a body violates hegemonic regimes of masculinity. To emphasise once again, the first encounter with gay culture for young gay men nowadays is usually online and so sites like this are, in many ways, reproducing the restrictive, normative and highly restrictive policing of gender regimes that children experience in schoolyard bullying. In this respect, far from being a blank canvas which can efface gender politics, the internet may well be yet another instrument in maintaining normative gender performances in contemporary culture. Debra Ferreday has argued that this occurs throughout online 'virtual communities' and so, despite the pervasive liberatory rhetoric of online cultures, she argues that 'websites and associated texts work to produce and maintain boundaries' which can 'marginalise some users while simultaneously producing a sense of belonging in others' (Ferreday 2009: 14).

Critics have also pointed out that the ways in which online communities reflect and reinforce existing social hierarchies of gender is also apparent in the politics of gaming. Online gaming is increasingly under scrutiny by scholars, journalists and participants for its particularly virulent form of aggressive, macho, homophobic, racist and misogynist culture (though, in keeping with the debates we looked at in Chapter 2, violent insults are often framed as 'ironic'). Nakamura explains that for some a particular version of white male 'geek' masculinity is established through the explicit denigration of those who fall outside its parameters and that gaming is a *crucial* site for the production of this identification. Nakamura argues that 'gaming capital is in fact *aspirational* for many young male players, as much a goal as it is a reality. Masculinity is performed by the display of technical knowledge, and gaming is the most recent iteration of this form of social display. Gaming itself becomes a mark of privilege within symbolic discourse' (Nakamura 2012). Nakamura cites the 2012 *New York Times* article which publicised details of Aris Bakhtanian's experiences of sexual harassment at the Cross Assault video game tournament (O'Leary 2012) and the experience of an African American actress Aisha Tyler, commenting that 'women of color gamers who publicly identify with the culture of gaming find themselves shunned, mocked, and generally treated in ways that are far worse than one could find in almost any other social context' (Nakamura 2012). She concludes that 'it is abundantly apparent that the more gaming capital becomes identified with white masculinity, the more bitter the battle over its distribution, possession, and circulation will become. As gaming culture becomes more heavily capitalized both economically and symbolically, it becomes both more important for women to gain positions of power as critics, makers, and players' (ibid.).

Trolling, Cyberbullying and Gender Regimes: The New Forums for Misogyny and Heteronormativity

Recent well-publicised accounts of online and cyber harassment, hate speech and trolling have demonstrated the ways in which the culture of new technologies and new formats are very much the 'front line' in terms of gender politics. Cyberbullying is a term which is used to describe the various ways that people experience intimidation, harassment and vilification online. Scholars have suggested that it is most usually used in relation to children and adolescents (Kowalski et al. 2008: 43). As we've already seen, recently the media have reported cyberbullying as linked to the deaths of teenagers both through blackmailing and through online abuse. In one sense cyberbullying can be understood as closely related to more 'traditional' sites and researchers have found that the perpetrators and victims of bullying tend to conform to profiles already understood by those working in education and social psychology. Researchers have identified that children with learning and physical disabilities, overweight children and 'adolescents who are gay, lesbian, or bisexual, those who may be questioning their sexuality, and those who may be perceived as "too feminine" (boys) or "too masculine" (girls) are more likely to be bullied' (ibid.: 26). This is a cross-cultural phenomenon, though, with specific cultural contours and differences amongst platforms. What is distinctive about cyberbullying, however, is arguably the insidiousness of the way it can reach into increasingly ubiquitous online space. In this respect, it is increasingly hard to escape and has a demonstrably wider 'reach' than, say, a note passed round amongst classmates. It is a term which covers a huge spectrum from one-off derogatory comments to flaming (hostile online attacks), stalking, 'happy slapping', harassment, denigration, outing and trickery (ibid.: 46–51). It is also a difficult term to define as it encompasses a range of both modalities and platforms (though these can be summed up as 'electronic communications technologies').

The dilemma that the anonymity, made possible by communication formats, poses should be understood in relation to the history of the ways in which these technologies evolved. E. Gabriella Coleman argues that to understand 'contemporary internet cultures – such as Internet trolling' it is important to consider their history and evolution and the links that are made to both so-called 'hacker ethics' and the conceptual space of the new technologies as a place of radical anti-authoritarianism:

> There is a rich aesthetic tradition of spectacle and transgression at play with trolls, which includes the irreverent legacy of phreakers [telecommunications trespassers] and the hacker underground. This aesthetic tradition demonstrates an important political attribute of spectacle: the marked hyperbole and spectacle among phreakers, hackers and trollers not only makes it difficult to parse out truth from lies; it has made it difficult to decipher and understand the cultural politics of their actions.
>
> (Coleman 2012: 101)

Whilst this qualification is clearly justified, the 'cultural politics' of trolling may indeed be hard to decipher and it would be quite wrong to attribute trolling only to misogynists, homophobes and racists. Nonetheless, it is also fair to say that gender and sexuality are one of the favoured battlegrounds of the new media. In the UK, recently, the case of Caroline Criado Perez highlights some of the more worrying aspects of online environments viewed from a gender perspective. In July 2013 Perez was instrumental in persuading the Bank of England that there was a problem with its new designs for UK currency in that none of the great British figures adorning the currency were women. The bank reconsidered and in July of 2013 they announced that Jane Austen would feature on the new £10 note. Caroline Perez was featured in a number of news broadcasts and newspapers over her role in the decision. Subsequent to these media appearances she received a large volume of threats, specifically rape threats. The failure of Twitter to take the threats seriously became another media story and the widespread use of misogynist language and 'trolling' was debated in the pages of the press, online and across the media. It was even addressed in Parliament as a result of other female journalists and politicians speaking out about everyday abuse, including graphic threats of sexual violence and even death threats. Future scholarship on gender and digital media will need to consider two questions. First, to what extent does the gendered nature of trolling become a concern, given that it is in some sense virtual rather than real? Second, is the inflammatory language used meant to be understood as playful, 'ironic' and entirely divorced from 'real life' and therefore immune to critique, despite being illegal?

In this chapter we have considered some of the work that looks at electronic communication and its diverse identificatory and gender politics. The picture that emerges is clearly a mixed one. Online environments offer the possibility for newly inflected gender identifications, though they are subject to some of the same, sometimes far from progressive, gender dynamics of the social worlds out of which they are created and in which they are immersed.

Conclusion

In this textbook we have aimed to introduce the key debates within the study of gender in the media. We commenced with a discussion about the difference between sex and gender, and then considered the ways in which gender politics have been mobilised to address these issues, before applying these cultural theories to a consideration of popular media texts. Central to these debates has been the argument that the media not only represents ideas of masculinity and femininity but that the very process of making images is, in itself, gendered. Visual culture – in particular film and television – maintains a gendered bias in the very art of spectatorship and the identification processes. The act of gazing at images is gendered and replicated throughout the discourses of film, television, advertising and online media. Most importantly, the ideas we maintain about ourselves – such as class, race and, most importantly, gender – do not just happen but are discursively constructed. A key discourse within this is the media, and it is fair to say that it has given us an idea of what it means to be gendered and to 'do' this gender on a daily basis.

However, we have also argued that it is naïve to assume that spectators simply absorb everything from the media without any form of interrogation or negotiation. Indeed, as we asserted in Chapter 1, this is a key element within feminist media criticism, which points out that the pleasure of texts should not be overlooked and that female spectators should not be reduced to passive ciphers who absorb – without question – all the images they see on the screen. Nevertheless, it is still very much the case that specific ideologies of masculinity and femininity are circulated in the media, both in the iconography of representations and within the very mechanism of representation itself.

Therefore, the key question to ask here is whether media representations of gender *are* changing. As we saw in Chapter 7, online media (especially interactive, virtual reality sites, such as chatrooms) do present the opportunity to move beyond hegemonic ideologies of gender and to challenge or queer gender hegemonies. Yet has this really happened? As more recent scholarship has asserted, online media seems to have reinforced conservative, if not even essentialist, ideas of gender and gender roles. More recently, as we argued in Chapters 2 and 4, we have seen 'ironic' representations of masculinity and femininity in a variety of media (especially television) as sensibilities such as metrosexuality and post-feminism have coloured and shaped a variety of representations. It does seem as if contemporary media representation is now cloaked in a veil of postmodern irony which allows ideologies to be conveyed but excuses anything which might be regressive, or repressive, through recourse to an ironic wink at the spectator. Are these texts unashamedly regressive – representing archaic ideologies of sexism and even misogyny – and merely disguising them with a veil of irony? Indeed, many media texts seem to say: 'this is sexist but because the text itself shows an awareness of this sexism then that is acceptable'. On the other hand, there is an argument to be made that these representations are premised upon the agreement that we now live in an 'enlightened' culture, in which an awareness of gender politics is apparent, and so media texts can afford to play with, toy with and even queer hegemonic gender roles.

Nevertheless, while many contemporary media texts and representations are playing with – even questioning – ideas of hegemonic masculinity and femininity, a question any spectator should ask is: how easily are these paradigms shifting towards everyday discourses? First of all, do all spectators 'get' the irony that is at work in these representations? Second, although television drama may (for example) represent a post-feminist or metrosexual 'paradise', are these politics really being mobilised in everyday life? For a great many people, gender ideologies are still enormously restrictive, and there are still schoolchildren being bullied because they fail to match up to expectations of masculinity and femininity. There are also grown men and women who fret about their gender performances as they sign up to an online dating gallery: am I masculine or feminine *enough*?

It is fair to say that we live in a culture in which ideologies do change – just not very fast. Hegemonic ideas of masculinity and femininity have, indeed, been rather constant for the past few centuries (for example, there have been relatively few matriarchal cultures in the world), though a negotiation and interrogation of these ideologies is starting to occur, if only, for most people, at an unconscious level – and it is the media which can be seen to play a considerable role in this. For example, the very popularity of make-over TV shows and online dating galleries is forcing spectators/participants to become aware (perhaps just at a subconscious level) of the way that culture constructs masculinity and femininity. Even the most passive of spectators, watching a make-over show, will realise that femininity is a particular 'doing' for which many of the participants need particular guidance along the path of their own personal project. In this respect, the media is surely helping to denaturalise gender ideologies and demonstrate their constructed nature, as opposed to reinforcing them.

However, this leads to the other key question: does revealing the constructedness of something actually do anything to challenge its autonomy? If we think about the history of power, where did the notion arise that the ruling classes or the dominant ideologies need to be *natural* in order to rule? Does exposing the constructed nature of gender roles and gender ideologies actually do anything to challenge these prescriptions? Even if people were now to say 'boys will be boys – but only with the guidance of media discourses', then that statement is still asserting that hegemonic masculinity *should* be maintained even if it is acknowledging that it is not natural or innate. In other words, far from assuming that a discussion of gender politics is no longer relevant for the contemporary student, we would assert that the necessity to interrogate, critique and, most importantly, reflect upon the gendered nature of media representation is now more important than ever.

We hope this textbook has introduced readers to the ways in which the media represents gender in a variety of texts and discourses. We have only given the briefest introduction to these fascinating debates but we hope they will inspire students to pursue particular topics in much more advanced, scholarly discussions. Most importantly, we hope this text will have opened our students' eyes to the power of gendered discourses in forming, transforming and shaping gendered identifications. Whether we are marvelling at a post-feminist utopia in a television drama, squirming in horror at the brutal gender policing of television make-over shows, in awe of the formation of celebrity bodies in the pages of glamorous magazines, or attempting to negotiate our gendered identifications online, we should ask ourselves if these representations have really moved us beyond our childhood years when we were playing with dolls and being instructed that boys *will* be boys and girls *will* be girls.

Bibliography

Adorno, Theodore (1991) 'The Schema of Mass Culture' in T. Adorno (ed.), *The Culture Industry: Selected Essays on Mass Culture*, ed. J.M. Bernstein (London: Routledge).

Akass, Kim and McCabe, Janet (eds) (2004) *Reading Sex and the City* (London: I.B.Tauris).

Allen, Dennis (2006) 'Making Over Masculinity: A Queer "I" for the Straight Guy', Genders.org, 44. available at http://genders.org/g44/g44_allen.html.

Ang, Ien (1991) *Living Room Wars: Rethinking Media Audiences for a Postmodern World* (London: Routledge).

Arthurs, Jane (2003) '*Sex and the City* and Consumer Culture: Re Mediating Postfeminist Drama', *Feminist Media Studies*, 3(1): 83–98.

Attwood, Feona (2009) 'Intimate Adventures: Sexblogs, Sexbooks and Women's Sexual Narration', *European Journal of Cultural Studies* 12(1): 5–20.

Bartky, Sandra Lee (1988) 'Feminism, Foucault and the Modernisation of Patriarchal Power', in Irene Diamond and Lee Quinby (eds) *Feminism and Foucault: Reflections on Resistance* (Boston: Northeastern University Press), pp. 61–86.

——— (1990) *Femininity and Domination: Studies in the Phenomenology of Oppression* (London: Routledge).

Battles, Kathleen and Hilton-Morrow, Wendy (2000) 'Gay Characters in Conventional Spaces: *Will and Grace* and the Situation Comedy Genre', *Critical Studies in Media Communication*, 19(1): 87–105.

Baudrillard, Jean (1983) *Simulations*, translated by Paul Foss, Paul Patton and Philip Beitchman (New York: Semiotext(e)).

Benwell, Bethan (2004) 'Ironic Discourse: Evasive Masculinity in Men's Lifestyle Magazines', *Men and Masculinities*, 7(1): 3–21.

Berger, John (1972) *Ways of Seeing* (Harmondsworth: Penguin Books).

Berila, Beth and Devika Dibya Choudhuri (2005) 'Metrosexuality the Middle Class Way: Exploring Race, Class and Gender in *Queer Eye for the Straight Guy*', Genders.org, 42, available at www.genders.org/g42_berila_choudhuri.html.

Bersani, Leo (1995) *Homos* (Cambridge, MA: Harvard University Press).

Blum, Virginia (2003) *Flesh Wounds: The Culture of Cosmetic Surgery* (Berkeley: University of California Press).

Bordo, Susan (1999) *The Male Body: A New Look at Men in Public and in Private* (New York: Farrar, Strauss and Giroux).

—— (2003) *Unbearable Weight: Feminism, Western Culture and the Body* (Berkeley: University of California Press).

Braidotti, Rosi (2002) 'The Use and Abuses of the Sex/Gender Distinction', in G. Griffin and R. Braidotti (eds), *Thinking Differently: A Reader in European Women's Studies* (London: Zed Books), pp. 285-307.

Brooks, Ann (1998) *Postfeminisms* (London: Routledge).

Bruckman, Amy (1992) 'Identity Workshops: Emergent Social and Psychological Phenomena in Text-based Virtual Reality', unpublished article available ftp at parcftp.xerox.com /pub/MOO/papers), MIT Media Laboratory, Cambridge, MA.

Brunsdon, Charlotte (1997) 'Identity in Feminist Television Criticism', in Charlotte Brunsdon, Julie D'Acci and Lynn Spigel (eds), *Feminist Television Criticism* (Oxford: Clarendon Press).

—— (2000) *The Feminist, The Housewife and the Soap Opera* (Oxford: Oxford University Press).

—— (2006) 'The Feminist in the Kitchen: Martha, Martha and Nigella' in Joanne Hollows and Rachel Moseley (eds), *Feminism in Popular Culture* (Oxford: Berg).

—— (2013) 'Television Crime Series, Women Police and Fuddy Duddy Feminism' *Feminist Media Studies* 13(3): 375-394.

—— and Spigel, Lynn (eds) (2008) *Feminist Television Criticism: A Reader*, 2nd edn (Maidenhead: Open University Press), 1st edn 1997.

Bruzzi, Stella (1997) *Undressing Cinema: Clothing and Identity in the Movies* (London and New York: Routledge).

—— and Church Gibson, Pamela (2004) '"Fashion is the Fifth Character": Fashion, Costume and Character in *Sex and the City*', in Kim Akass and Janet McCabe (eds) *Reading Sex and the City* (London: I.B.Tauris).

Butler, Jeremy G. (1998) 'The Star System and Hollywood' in J. Hill and P. Church Gibson (eds), *The Oxford Guide to Film Studies* (Oxford: Oxford University Press), pp. 342-54.

Butler, Judith (1990) *Gender Trouble: Feminism and the Subversion of Identity* (London and New York: Routledge).

—— (1993) *Bodies that Matter: On the Discursive Limits of Sex* (London and New York: Routledge).

Byerly, Carolyn, M. and Ross, Karen (2006) *Women and Media: A Critical Introduction* (Maldon,MA and Oxford: Blackwell).

Carter, Cynthia and Steiner, Linda (eds) (2004) *Critical Readings: Media and Gender* (Maidenhead, Open University Press).

CEOP (Child Exploitation and Online Protection) (2013) 'Threat Assessment of Child Sexual Abuse', child exploitation and online protection centre report available at: www.ceop.police.uk/Documents/peopdocs/pEOP_TACSEA2013_240613%20FINAL.pdf.

Chapman, Rowena (1988) 'The Great Pretender: Variations on the New Man Theme' in R. Chapman and J. Rutherford (eds) *Male Order: Unwrapping Masculinity* (London: Lawrence & Wishart).

—— and Rutherford, Jonathan (1988) *Male Order: Unwrapping Masculinity* (London: Lawrence & Wishart).

Closer (2011) 20–26 August.

Cochrane, K. (2009) 'A Woman's World' *The Guardian*, 5 May.

Coleman, E. Gabriella (2012) 'Phreaks, Hackers, and Trolls: The Politics of Transgression and Spectacle' in M. Mandiberg (ed.) *The Social Media Reader* (New York: New York University Press), pp. 99–119.

Coles, Fen (1999) 'Feminist Charms and Outrageous Arms' in Janet Price and Margrit Shildrick (eds.) *Feminist Theory and the Body: A Reader* (Edinburgh: Edinburgh University Press).

Connell, Raewyn (1987) 'Hegemonic Masculinity and Emphasized Femininity', in her *Gender and Power* (Sydney: Allen & Unwin), pp. 183–89.

Connor, Steve (2001) 'The Shame of Being a Man', *Textual Practice*, 15(2).

Copjec, Joan (1989) 'The Orthopsychic Subject: Film Theory and the Reception of Lacan', *October*, 49: 53–71.

Couldry, Nick (2003) *Media Rituals: A Critical Approach* (London and New York: Routledge).

Croners, Jen (2011) 'Who's a Big Boy then Becks?', *heat magazine*, 20–26 August. 3.

Dahlberg, Lincoln (2001) 'The Habermasian Public Sphere Encounters Cyber-Reality', *Critical Review*, 8(3).

Daily Mail (2011) 'Curvy Mad Men Star Christina Hendricks Fuels Demand for Breast Enlargements', 30 January, available at: www.dailymail.co.uk/femail/article-1351890/Mad-Men-star-Christina-Hendricks-fuels-demand-breast-enlargements.html.

Davis, Kathy (2002) 'A Dubious Equality: Men, Women and Cosmetic Surgery', *Body & Society*, 8(1): 49–65.

de Beauvoir, Simone (1949) *The Second Sex* (New York: Vintage).

de Cordova, R. (1991) 'The Emergence of the Star System in America', in Christine Gledhill (ed.) *Stardom: Industry of Desire* (London: Routledge).

Dickel, Michael H. (1996) 'Bent Gender: Virtual Disruptions of Gender and Sexual Identity', *Electronic Journal of Communication*, 5: 95–117.

Doane, Mary Ann (1982) 'Film and the Masquerade: Theorising the Female Spectator' *Screen* 23(3–4): 74–88.

Doyle, S. (2009) 'Mad Men's Feminine Mystique' *The Guardian*, 15 August, available at: www.theguardian.com/pommentisfree/pifamerica/2009/aug/15/mad-men-season-three-feminism-television.

Dyer, Richard (1982) 'Don't Look Now: The Male Pin-Up', *Screen* 23, (3–4): 61–7

—— (1998) *Stars* (London: BFI).

—— (2004) *Heavenly Bodies: Film Stars and Society*, 2nd edn (London: Routledge), 1st edn 1986.

Elsaesser, Thomas (1987) ' Tales of Sound and Fury Observations on the Family Melodrama' ,in Christine Gledhill (ed.), *Home is Where the Heart is: Studies in Melodrama and the Woman's Film* (London: BFI).

Feasey, Rebecca (2006) 'Get a Famous Body: Star Styles and Celebrity Gossip in *heat magazine*', in Debra Ferreday (2009) *Online Belongings: Fantasy, Affect and Web Communities* (Bern: Peter Lang).

Foster, Thomas (2001) 'Trapped by the Body? Telepresence Technologies and Transgendered Performance in Feminist and Lesbian Rewriting of Cyberpunk Fiction' in David Bell and Barbara M. Kennedy (eds) *The Cybercultures Reader* (London: Routledge), pp. 539–459.

Foucault, Michel (1977) *Discipline and Punish: The Birth of the Prison* (New York: Random House).

Friedan, Betty (2001) *The Feminine Mystique* (New York: Norton).

Gamman, Lorraine. and Marshment, Margaret (eds)(1988) *The Female Gaze: Women as Viewers of Popular Culture* (London: Women's Press).

Genz, Stephanie and Brabon, Benjamin (2009) *Postfeminism Cultural Texts and Theories* (Edinburgh: Edinburgh University Press).

Gerhard, Jane (2005) '*Sex and the City*: Carrie Bradshaw's Queer Postfeminism', *Feminist Media Studies* 5(1): 37–49.

Gill, Rosalind (2007) *Gender and the Media* (Cambridge: Polity Press).

Grazia (2011) issue 29 August.

Guthrie, Sharon and Castelnuovo, Shirley (1992) 'Elite Women Bodybuilders: Models of Resistance or Compliance?' *Play and Culture*, 5: 401–408.

Halberstam, Judith (1998) *Female Masculinity* (Durham: Duke University Press).

Hansen-Miller, David, and Gill, Rosalind (2011) '"Lad Flicks": Discursive Reconstructions of Masculinity in Popular Film' in Hilary Radner and Rebecca Stringer (eds) *Feminism at the Movies: Understanding Gender in Contemporary Popular Cinema* (New York and London: Routledge).

Haraway, Donna (1991) '"Gender" for a Marxist Dictionary: The Sexual Politics of a Word", *Simians, Cyborgs and Women: The Reinvention of Nature* (London: Free Association Books), pp. 127–48.

Hare, D. (2010) 'Mad Men: The Future of American Film Is on Television – Mad Men's Immaculate Re-creation of Another Way of Life Reminds Us Vividly of our Own', *The Guardian*, 8 September, available at: www.theguardian.com/tv-and-radio/2010/sep/08/mad-men-david-hare.

Heller, Dana (2007) *Makeover Television: Realities Remodelled* (London: I.B Tauris).

Hello! (2011) issue 1189, 29 August 2011.

Hermes, J. (1997) *Reading Women's Magazines* (Cambridge: Polity Press).

Herring, Susan C and Martinson, Anna (2004) 'Assessing Gender Authenticity in Computer-Mediated Language Use: Evidence from an Identity Game', *Journal of Language and Social Psychology*, December (23) 4: 424–46.

Heyes, Cressida (2007) 'Cosmetic Surgery and the Televisual Makeover: A Foucauldian Feminist Reading', *Feminist Media Studies*, 7(1): 17–32.

—— and Jones, Meredith (eds) (2009) *Cosmetic Surgery: A Feminist Primer* (Farnham: Ashgate Publishing).

Hill, Emily (2010) ' A Damaging Dream of *Mad Men*'s Joan', *The Guardian*, Tuesday 27 July, 2010 available at: http://www.theguardian.com/commentis-free/2010/jul/27/lynne-featherstone-mad-men-joan.

Hine, Christine (2000) *Virtual Ethnography* (London: Sage).

Hollows, Joanne (2000) *Feminism, Femininity and Popular Culture* (Manchester: Manchester University Press).

—— (2006) 'Can I Go Home Yet? Feminism, Post-feminism and Domesticity', in Joanne Hollows and Rachel Moseley (eds) *Feminism in Popular Culture* (Oxford: Berg) 97–118.

—— and Moseley, Rachel (2006) 'Popularity Contests: The Meanings of Popular Feminism' in Joanne Hollows and Rachel Moseley (eds) *Feminism in Popular Culture* (Oxford: Berg).

Holmes, Su (2005) 'Off guard, Unkempt, Unready? Deconstructing Contemporary Celebrity in *heat* Magazine', *Continuum: Journal of Media and Cultural Studies* 19(1): 21–38.

—— and Redmond, Sean (eds) (2006) *Framing Celebrity* (London: Routledge).

hooks, bell (1994) *Outlaw Culture: Resisting Representations* (London: Routledge).

—— (1996) *Reel to Real Race Sex and Class at the Movies* (New York: Routledge).

Huyssen, Andreas (1988) *After the Great Divide: Modernism, Mass Culture and Postmodernism* (Basingstoke: Macmillan).

Jagose, Annamarie (1996) *Queer Theory* (Melbourne: Melbourne University Press).

Jeffords, Susan (1994) *Hard Bodies: Hollywood Masculinity in the Reagan Era* (New Jersey: Rutgers University Press).

Jermyn, Deborah (2004) 'In Love with Sarah Jessica Parker: Celebrating Female Fandom and Friendship in *Sex and the City*' in Kim Akass and Janet McCabe (eds) *Reading Sex and the City* (London: I.B.Tauris).

—— (2010) *Prime Suspect* (London: BFI/Palgrave Macmillan).

Jones, Owen (2011) *Chavs: The Demonization of the Working Class* (London: Verso)

Jordan, Tim (1999) *Cyberpower: The Cultural Politics of Cyberspace and the Internet* (London and New York: Routledge).

Kaplan, Daniels A. and Benét, J. (eds) (1978) *Hearth and Home Images of Women in the Mass Media* (Oxford: Oxford University Press).

Karlsson, L. (2007) 'Desperately Seeking Sameness' *Feminist Media Studies*, 7(2).

Kendall, Lori (1998) 'Meaning and Identity in "Cyberspace": The Performance of Gender, Class, and Race Online', *Symbolic Interaction* 21(2): 129–153.

Kowalski, Robin, Limber, Susan, and Agatston, Patricia (2008) *Cyberbullying, Bullying in the Digital Age* (Maldon, MA: Blackwell).

Kuhn, Annette (1994) *Women's Pictures: Feminism and Cinema* (London: Verso).

Lauzen, Martha (2008) 'Women @ the box office: a study of the top 100 worldwide grossing films', available at: http://womenintvfilm.sdsu.edu/research.html.

—— (2012) 'It's a Man's (Celluloid) World: on-screen representations of female characters in the top 100 films of 2011', available at: http://womenintvfilm.sdsu.edu/research.html.

—— (2013) 'The Celluloid Ceiling: behind-the-scenes employment of women in the top 250 films of 2012', available at: http://womenintvfilm.sdsu.edu/research.html.

Livingstone, S., Kirwil, L., Ponte, C., and Staksrud, E. (2013) *In Their Own Words: What Bothers Children Online?* (London: London School of Economics and Political Science) available at: http://eprints.lse.ac.uk/48357/.

Locks, Adam, and Richardson, Niall (eds) (2011) *Critical Readings in Bodybuilding* (London: Routledge).

Mackinnon, Kenneth (1997) *Uneasy Pleasures: The Male as Erotic Object* (London: Cygnus Arts).

Mandiberg, Michael (ed.) (2012) *The Social Media Reader* (New York: New York University Press).

Marshall, David (1997) *Celebrity and Power: Fame in Contemporary Culture* (Minneapolis: University of Minnesota Press).

Martison, M. (2012) 'Mad Men: It's All about the Women Now', *The Guardian*, 26 March, available at: www.theguardian.com/lifeandstyle/the-womens-blog-with-jane-martinson/2012/mar/26/mad-men-about-women-now.

McCrae, Shannon (1997) 'Flesh Made Word: Sex, Text and the Virtual Body' in D. Porter (ed.), *Internet Culture* (London: Routledge), pp. 73–86.

Mclean, G. (2009) 'Is Mad Men Misogynistic?', *The Guardian*, 21 May, available at: www.theguardian.com/pulture/garethmcleanblog+tv-and-radio/mad-men-tv-series.

McRobbie, Angela (2007) 'Postfeminism and Popular Culture: Bridget Jones and the New Gender Regime' in Yvonne Tasker and Diane Negra (eds) *Interrogating Postfeminism: Gender and the Politics of Popular Culture* (Durham: Duke University Press).

——— (2004) 'Notes on *What Not to Wear* and post-feminist symbolic violence', in L. Adkins and B. Skeggs (eds), *Feminism after Bourdieu* (Oxford: Blackwell).

——— (2009) *The Aftermath of Feminism* (London: Sage).

Mellencamp, Patricia (1992) *High Anxiety: Catastrophe, Scandal, Age and Comedy* (Bloomington: Indiana University Press).

Mendelson, A. and Papacharissi, Z. (2011) 'Look at Us: Collective Narcissism in College Student Facebook Photo Galleries' in Z. Papacharissi (ed.) *A Networked Self: Identity, Community and Culture on Social Networking Sites* (New York: Routledge), pp. 251–73.

Merck, Mandy (2004) 'Sexuality in the City', in Kim Akass and Janet McCabe (eds) *Reading Sex and the City* (London: I.B.Tauris).

Meyer, Richard (1991) 'Rock Hudson's Body' in Diana Fuss (ed.) *Inside/Out: Lesbian Theories, Gay Theories* (London: Routledge).

Milestone, Katie and Meyer, Anneke (2012) *Gender and Popular Culture* (London: Polity).

Miller, Toby (2005) 'A Metrosexual Eye on Queer Guy', *Gay and Lesbian Quarterly*, 11(1): 112–17.

Mitchell, Juliet (1975) *Psychoanalysis and Feminism* (New York: Vintage Books).

Modleski, Tanya (1988) *Loving with a Vengeance: Mass Produced Fantasies for Women* (New York and London: Routledge).

Morgan, Kathryn Pauly (1991) 'Women and the Knife: Cosmetic Surgery and the Colonization of Women's Bodies', *Hypatia*, 6(3): 25.

Mort, Frank (1988) 'Boy's Own: Masculinity, Style and Popular Culture' in R. Chapman and J. Rutherford *Male Order: Unwrapping Masculinity* (London: Lawrence & Wishart).

Moseley, Rachel (2002) 'Glamorous Witchcraft: Gender and Magic in Teen Film and Television', *Screen* 43(4): 403–422.

Mowlabocus, Sharif (2009) 'Revisiting Old Haunts Through New Technologies: Public (Homo)Sexual Cultures in Cyberspace', *International Journal of Cultural Studies* 11(4): 419–439.

—— (2010) *Gaydar Culture: Gay Men, Technology and Embodiment in the Digital Age* (Hampshire: Ashgate).

Mulvey, Laura (1975) 'Visual Pleasure and Narrative Cinema' reprinted in L. Mulvey (1989) *Visual and Other Pleasures* (Basingstoke: Macmillan).

—— (1989) *Visual and Other Pleasures* (Basingstoke: Macmillan).

—— (1987) 'Notes on Sirk and Melodrama' in Gledhill, Christine ed. *Home is Where the Heart is: Studies in Melodrama and the Woman's Film* (London: BFI).

Munt, Sally (2007) *Queer Attachments: The Cultural Politics of Shame* (Farnham: Ashgate).

Nakamura, L. (2012) 'Queer Female of Color: The Highest Difficulty Setting There Is? Gaming Rhetoric as Gender Capital', *Ada: A Journal of Gender, New Media, and Technology* 1, available at: http://adanewmedia.org/2012/11/issue1-naka-mura/.

Neale, Steve (1993) 'Masculinity as Spectacle: Reflections on Men and Mainstream Cinema', in Steven Cohan and Ina Rae Hard (eds) *Screening the Male: Exploring Masculinities in Hollywood Cinema* (London and New York: Routledge), first published in *Screen* (1983).

Negra, Diane (2001) *Off White Hollywood: American Culture and Ethnic Female Stardom* (London: Routledge).

—— (2004) 'Quality Postfeminism? Sex and the Single Girl on HBO' *Genders*, 39.

—— (2009) *What a Girl Wants? Fantasizing the Reclamation of Self in Postfeminism* (London: Routledge).

Nietzsche, Friedrich (1996 [1887]) *On the Genealogy of Morals (Zur Genealogie der Moral)*, trans. Douglas Smith (Oxford: Oxford University Press).

Nixon, Sean (1996) *Hard Looks: Masculinities, Spectatorship and Contemporary Consumption* (London: UCL Press).

—— (2001) 'Resignifying Masculinity: From "New Man" to "New Lad"' in David Morley and Kevin Robins (eds) *British Cultural Studies: Geography, Nationality and Identity* (Oxford: Oxford University Press).

O'Leary, Amy,(2012) 'In Virtual Play Sex Harassment is All Too Real' *New York Times* August 1 2012, available at: http://www.nytimes.com/2012/08/02/us/sexual-harassment-in-online-gaming-stirs-anger.html?_r=0.

Oliver, Harriet (2010) 'News and Shoes: femininity, consumption and journalistic professional identity', unpublished PhD thesis, Goldsmiths, University of London.

Papacharissi, Zizi (ed.) (2011) *A Networked Self: Identity, Community and Culture on Social Networking Sites* (New York: Routledge).

Parker, Andrew (1996) 'The Construction of Masculinity within Boys' Physical Education', *Gender and Education*, 8: 141–57.

Pascoe, Cheri J. (2005) '"Dude, You're a Fag": Adolescent Masculinity and the Fag Discourse', *Sexualities*, 8(3): 329–46.

Poster, Mark (1995) *The Second Media Age* (Cambridge: Polity Press).

Power, M. (2012) 'How to Drive Men Mad', *Daily Mail*, 31 March, available at: www.dailymail.co.uk/femail/article-2122982/Mad-Men-makeover-You-work-hard-wolf-whistles.html.

Projansky, Sarah (2001) *Watching Rape: Film and Television in Postfeminist Culture* (New York: New York University Press).

Rellstab, Daniel H. (2007) 'Staging gender online: gender plays in Swiss internet relay chats', *Discourse & Society* 18(6): 765–787.

Rheingold, Howard (1993) *Virtual Community: Finding Connection in a Computerized World* (London: Minerva Press).

Richardson, Niall (2003) 'Effeminophobia', *AXM*, February.

—— (2004) 'The Gospel According to Spiderman', *Journal of Popular Culture*, 37(4).

—— (2006) 'As Kamp as Bree: The Politics of Camp Reconsidered by *Desperate Housewives*', *Feminist Media Studies* 6(2).

—— (2008a) 'Flex Rated! Female Bodybuilding: Feminist Resistance or Erotic Spectacle?', *Journal of Gender Studies*, 17(4): 289–301.

—— (2008b) *The Queer Cinema of Derek Jarman: Critical and Cultural Readings* (London: I.B.Tauris).

—— (2009) 'Effeminophobia, Misogyny and Queer Friendship: The Cultural Themes of Channel 4's *Playing it Straight*', *Sexualities*, 12:4.

—— (2010) *Transgressive Bodies: Representations in Film and Popular Culture* (Farnham: Ashgate).

——, Smith, Clarissa, and Werndly, Angela (2013) *Studying Sexualities: Theories, Representations, Practices* (London: Palgrave Macmillan).

Roberts, M. (2007) 'The Fashion Police: Governing the Self in What Not to Wear', in Y. Tasker and D. Negra (eds), *Interrogating Postfeminism: Gender and the Politics of Popular Culture* (Durham: Duke University Press).

Rojek, Chris (2001) *Celebrity* (London: Reaktion).

Rose, Jacqueline (1983) 'Femininity and its Discontents', *Feminist Review*, 80; reprinted 2005.

—— (1986) 'Feminine Sexuality: Jacques Lacan and the *école freudienne*', in J. Rose(ed.), *Sexuality in the Field of Vision* (London: Verso).

—— (2003) 'The Cult of Celebrity', in Rose, Jacqueline *On Not Being Able to Sleep: Psychoanalysis and the Modern World* (Princeton, NJ: Princeton University Press).

Rubin, Gayle (1975) 'The Traffic in Women: Notes on the "Political Economy" of Sex', in R. Reiter (ed.), *Toward an Anthropology of Women* (New York: Monthly Review Press), pp. 157-210.

Russo, Vito (1981) *The Celluloid Closet: Homosexuality in the Movies* (New York: Harper & Row).

Sedgwick, Eve Kosofsky (1985) *Between Men: English Literature and Male Homosocial Desire* (New York: Columbia University Press).

—— (1990) *Epistemology of the Closet* (Berkeley: University of California Press)

—— (1998) 'A Dialogue on Love', *Critical Inquiry*, 24 (Winter).

Segal, Lynne (1990) *Slow Motion: Changing Masculinities, Changing Men* (London: Virago).

Seidman, Steven (ed.) (1996) *Queer Theory/Sociology* (Oxford: Blackwell).

Shohat, E. and Stam, R. (1994) *Unthinking Eurocentrism: Multiculturalism and the Media* (London: Routledge).

Shriver, L. (2010) 'Beautiful Betty: A Warning from Home-making History' *The Guardian*, 10 March, available at: www.theguardian.com/commentis-free/2010/mar/10/petty-mad-men-feminine-mystique.

Shugart, Helene A. (2003) 'Reinventing Privilege: The New (Gay) Man in Contemporary Popular Media', *Critical Studies in Media Communication*, 20(1): 67–91.

Sinfield, Alan (1994) *The Wilde Century: Effeminacy, Oscar Wilde and the Queer Moment* (London: Cassell).

Skeggs, Beverly (2004) *Class, Self, Culture* (London: Routledge).

Smith, Clarissa (2007) *One for the Girls: The Pleasures and Practices of Reading Women's Porn* (Bristol: Intellect).

Spelman, Elizabeth (1982) 'Woman as Body: Ancient and Contemporary Views', *Feminist Studies*, 8(1): 108–131.

St Martin, Leena and Gavey, Nicola (1996) 'Women's Bodybuilding: Feminist Resistance and/or Femininity's Recuperation?', *Body and Society*, 2(4): 45–57.

Stacey, Jackie (1994) *Star Gazing: Hollywood Cinema and Female Spectatorship* (London: Routledge).

Stone, Allucquère Rosanne (2000) 'Will the Real Body Please Stand Up? Boundary Stories about Virtual Cultures' in David Bell and Barbara Kennedy (eds), *The Cybercultures Reader* (London: Routledge).

Tasker, Yvonne (1993) *Spectacular Bodies: Gender, Genre and the Action Cinema* (London: Routledge).

Tasker, Yvonne and Negra, Diane (2005) 'In Focus: Postfeminism and Contemporary Media Studies', *Cinema Journal* ,44.2: 107–10.

——(2007) *Interrogating Postfeminism: Gender and the Politics of Popular Culture* (Durham: Duke University Press).

Taylor, A. (2011) 'Blogging Solo: New Media, "Old" Politics', *Feminist Review* 99(1): 79–97.

Thornham, Sue (1999) (ed.) *Feminist Film Theory* (Edinburgh: Edinburgh University Press).

—— (2000) *Feminist Theory and Cultural Studies: Stories of Unsettled Relations* (London: Hodder Arnold).

—— and Purvis, Tony (2005) *Television Drama Theories and Identities* (Basingstoke: Palgrave Macmillan).

—— and Richardson, Niall (2013) *Film and Gender* (London: Routledge).

Tincknell, Estella (2005) *Mediating the Family: Gender, Culture and Representation* (London: Hodder Education).

Truth, Sojourner (1995) 'Ain't I a Woman', in Beverly Guy-Sheftall (ed.) *Words of Fire: An Anthology of African-American Feminist Thought* (New York: The New Press).

Tuchman, Gaye (1978) 'The Symbolic Annihilation of Women by the Mass Media' in Tuchman, G., Kaplan Daniels, A. and Benét, J (eds) (1978) *Hearth and Home Images of Women in the Mass Media* (New York: Oxford University Press).

Turkle, Sherrie (1995) *Life on the Screen: Identity in the Age of the Internet* (New York: Simon & Schuster).

Turner, Graham (2004) *Understanding Celebrity* (London: Sage).

Tyler, Imogen (2001) 'Skin Tight: Celebrity, Pregnancy and Subjectivity', in Sara Ahmed and Jackie Stacey (eds) *Thinking Through the Skin* (London: Routledge) *Vanity Fair* (2011) Issue September.

Van Zoonen, Liesbet (1994) *Feminist Media Studies* (London: Sage).

Warner, Michael (ed.) (1993) *Fear of a Queer Planet: Queer Politics and Social Theory* (Minneapolis: University of Minnesota Press).

Wearing, Sadie (2007) 'Subjects of Rejuvenation: Aging in Postfeminist Culture' in Yvonne Tasker and Diane Negra (eds), *Interrogating Postfeminism: Gender and the Politics of Popular Culture* (Durham: Duke University Press), pp. 277–310.

—— (2011) 'Notes on Some Scandals: The Politics of Shame in *Vers le Sud*' in Rosalind Gill and Christina Scharff (eds), *New Femininities: Postfeminism, Neoliberalism and Identity* (Basingstoke: Palgrave Macmillan), pp. 173–187.

Weber, Brenda (2005) 'Beauty, Desire and Anxiety: The Economy of Sameness in ABC's Extreme Make-Over', Genders.org, 41, available at: www.genders.org/g41/g41_weber.html.

Whannel, Gary (2001) *Media Sports Stars Masculinities and Morality* (London: Routledge).

Whelehan, Immelda (2000) *Overloaded: Popular Culture and the Future of Feminism* (London: The Women's Press).

Whitehorn, K. (2009) 'Those Bras Were Made for Burning', *The Guardian*, 2 February, available at: www.theguardian.com/pulture/2009/feb/03/katharine-whitehorn-sexism-mad-m.

Willemen, Paul (1981) 'Anthony Mann: Looking at the Male', *Framework*, (5–17): 16–20.

Young, Lola (1996) *Fear of the Dark: 'Race' Gender and Sexuality in the Cinema* (London: Routledge).

Index

Printed and bound by CPI Group (UK) Ltd, Croydon, CR0 4YY